The Sayings of Confucius

CONFUCIUS

Translated by

LEONARD A. LYALL

The Sayings of Confucius

© Copyright 2010

Published by Timeless Classic Books

www.TimelessClassicBooks.net

ISBN 9-781453-881941

Introduction

Confucius was born in the year 550 B.C.,[1] in the land of Lu, in a small village, situated in the western part of the modern province of Shantung. His name was K'ung Ch'iu, and his style (corresponding to our Christian name) was Chung-ni. His countrymen speak of him as K'ung Fu-tzu, the Master, or philosopher K'ung. This expression was altered into Confucius by the Jesuit missionaries who first carried his fame to Europe.

Since the golden days of the Emperors Yao and Shun, the legendary founders of the Chinese Empire, nearly two thousand years had passed. Shun chose as his successor Yü, who had been his chief minister, a man whose devotion to duty was such that when engaged in draining the empire of the great flood—a task that took eight years to accomplish—he never entered his home till the work was done, although in the course of his labours he had thrice to pass his door. He founded the Hsia dynasty, which lasted till 1766 B.C. The last emperor of this line, a vile tyrant, was overthrown by T'ang, who became the first ruler of the house of Shang, or Yin. This dynasty again degenerated in course of time and came to an end in Chou, or Chou Hsin (1154-22 B.C.), a monster of lust, extravagance, and cruelty. The empire was only held together by the strength and wisdom of the Duke of Chou, or King Wen, to give him his popular title, one of the greatest men in Chinese history. He controlled two-thirds of the empire; but, believing that the people were not yet ready for a change, he refrained from dethroning the emperor. In his day 'the husbandman paid one in nine; the pay of the

---

[1] According to the great historian Ssu-ma Ch'ien. Other authorities say, 552 and 551 b.c.

officers was hereditary; men were questioned at barriers and at markets, but there were no tolls; fishgarths were not preserved; the children of criminals were sackless. The old and wifeless—the widower; the old and husbandless—the widow; the old and childless—the lone one; the young and fatherless—the orphan; these four are the people most in need below heaven, and they have no one to whom to cry, so when King Wen reigned his love went out first to them' (Mencius, Book II, chapter 5). After his death, his son, King Wu, decided that the nation was ripe for change. He overcame Chou Hsin by force of arms, and, placing himself on the throne, became the founder of the Chou dynasty.

In the time of Confucius the Chou dynasty still filled the throne. But it had long since become effete, and all power had passed into the hands of the great vassals. The condition of China was much like that of Germany in the worst days of the Holy Roman Empire. The emperor was powerless, the various vassal states were independent in all but name, and often at war one with the other. These states again were disintegrated, and their rulers impotent against encroaching feudatories. In Confucius' native state, Lu, the duke was a mere shadow. The younger branches of his house had usurped all power. Three in number, they were called the Three Clans. The most important of the three was the Chi, or Chi-sun clan, whose chiefs Chi Huan and Chi K'ang are often mentioned by Confucius. But the power of the Chi, too, was ill-secured. The minister Yang Huo overawed his master, and once even threw him into prison. Nor was the condition of the other states of the empire better than that of Lu. Confucius thought it worse.

Into this turbulent world Confucius was born. Though his father was only a poor military officer, he could trace his descent from the imperial house of Yin. Confucius married at nineteen, and is known to have had one son and one daughter. Shortly after his marriage he entered the service of the state as keeper of the granary. A year later he was put in charge of the public fields. In 527 B.C. his mother died, and, in obedience to Chinese custom, he had to retire from public life. When the years of mourning were over, he did not again take office, but devoted himself instead to study and teaching. As the years rolled by his fame grew, and a band of pupils gathered round him. In 517 B.C. the anarchy in Lu reached such a pitch that Confucius moved to the neighbouring land of Ch'i. Here he had several interviews with the reigning duke, but met with little encouragement (XVIII. 3). So he soon returned to his native country, and resumed for fifteen years his work as student and teacher.

During these fifteen years the power of the duke sank lower and lower, and the Chi was menaced by his minister Yang Huo. In times so dark, men that loved quiet sought in the world of thought an escape from the gloom around them, whilst others that were less resigned turned over in their minds the causes of the realm's decay. Lao-tzu, the founder of the mystic Taoist philosophy, taught that in inaction alone peace can be found; Mo-tzu proclaimed the doctrine of universal love: that we should love all men as we love self, love the parents of others as we love our own parents. Upright men were driven or fled from the world. Confucius often met them in his wanderings, and was reproved for not doing as they did. But his practical mind told him that inaction could not help the world, and that to find a remedy for the nation's ills, their cause must first be learned. This could only be done by historical study. He therefore devoted himself to the study of past times, edited in later life the *Book of History*, and compiled the work called *Spring and Autumn*, a history of his native state from 722 to 481 B.C. To bring again the golden days of Yao and Shun a return must be made to the principles of Wen and Wu, the kings that had rebuilt the empire after tyranny and selfishness had laid it low. Of impracticable ideals and renunciation of the world no good could come.

At last in 501 B.C. Yang Huo was forced to flee from Lu, and prospects brightened. A year later Confucius was appointed governor of a town. So great was his success as governor that before long he was promoted to be Superintendent of Works, and then to be Chief Criminal Judge. He won great influence with his master, and did much to lighten the general misery. He so strengthened the power of the duke that neighbouring states grew jealous. To sow dissension between duke and minister the men of Ch'i sent the duke a gift of singing girls. Such joy they gave him that for three days no court was held. On this Confucius left the land, 497 B.C.

For the next thirteen years Confucius wandered from land to land, followed by his disciples, seeking in vain for a ruler that was willing to employ him, and whom he was willing to serve. At times he was exposed to danger, at other times to want. But as a rule he was treated with consideration, although his teachings were ignored. Yet thirteen years of homeless wandering, of hopes deferred and frustrated, must have been hard to bear. When he left office Confucius was already fifty-three years old, and his life so far seemed a failure. The sense of his wasted powers may well have tempted him now and again to take office under an unworthy ruler; but knowing that no good could come of it he refrained, and probably he never seriously thought of doing so.

In 483 B.C., when Confucius was sixty-six years old, through the influence of his disciple Jan Yu, who was in the service of the Chi, the Master was invited to return to his native land. Here he remained till his death in 479 B.C. He had many interviews with the reigning duke and the head of the Chi clan, but gained no influence over either of them. So he turned once more to his favourite studies; edited the *Book of Poetry*—perhaps the most interesting collection of ancient songs extant—and wrote *Spring and Autumn*. His closing years were darkened by the loss of those dearest to him. First his son died, then Yen Yüan, the disciple whom he loved best. At his death the Master was overcome by grief, and he left none behind him that loved learning. Lastly Tzu-lu, the frank and bold, was killed in battle. A little later, in his seventy-first year, Confucius himself passed away, 479 B.C.

This book of the Master's Sayings is believed by the Chinese to have been written by the disciples of Confucius. But there is nothing to prove this, and some passages in the book point the other way. Book VIII speaks of the death of Tseng-tzu, who did not die till 437 B.C., forty-two years after the Master. The chief authority for the text as it stands to-day is a manuscript found in the house of Confucius in 150 B.C., hidden there, in all likelihood, between the years 213 and 211 B.C., when the reigning emperor was seeking to destroy every copy of the classics. We find no earlier reference to the book under its present name. But Mencius (372-289 B.C.) quotes seven passages from it, in language all but identical with the present text, as the words of Confucius. No man ever talked the language of these sayings. Such pith and smoothness is only reached by a long process of rounding and polishing. We shall probably come no nearer to the truth than Legge's conclusion that the book was put together by the pupils of the disciples of Confucius, from the words and notebooks of their masters, about the year 400 B.C.

Note

Such information as seemed necessary to enable the reader to understand the text, or that appeared to me to be of general interest, I have given in the notes at the foot of the page. Further details about the men and places mentioned in the text will be found in the Index.

Dates I have taken from Legge, Hirth and other standard authors.

In Chinese names, consonants are generally pronounced as in English, vowels as in Italian.

E, when not joined with *i*, is pronounced nearly as German *ö*, or much as *u* in English lu*c*k.

ao	rhymes	approximately	with	how
ei	"	"	"	they
ou	"	"	"	though
uo	"	"	"	poor,

the *u* being equivalent to *w*.

Chih and *Shih* rhyme approximately with *her*. *Tzu* is pronounced much as *sir* in the vulgar *yessir*, but with a hissing sound prefixed.

Contents

The Sayings of Confucius

Book I

1. The Master said, To learn and then do, is not that a pleasure? When friends come from afar do we not rejoice? To live unknown and not fret, is not that to be a gentleman?
2. Yu-tzu[2] said. Few men that are good sons and good brothers are fond of withstanding those over them. A man that is not fond of withstanding those over him and is yet fond of broils is nowhere found. A gentleman heeds the roots. When the root has taken, the Way is born. And to be a good son and a good brother, is not that the root of love?
3. The Master said, Smooth words and fawning looks are seldom found with love.
4. Tseng-tzu[3] said, Thrice daily I ask myself: In dealing for others, have I been unfaithful? Have I been untrue to friends? Do I practise what I preach?
5. The Master said, To guide a land of a thousand chariots, honour business and be true; spend little and love men; time thy calls on the people.
6. The Master said, The young should be dutiful at home, modest abroad, careful and true, overflowing in kindness for all, but in brotherhood with love. And if they have strength to spare they should spend it on the arts.

---

[2] A disciple
[3] A disciple

7. Tzu-hsia[4] said, If a man eschews beauty and honours worth, if he serves his father and mother with all his strength, if he is ready to give his life for his lord, and keeps faith with his friends, though others may say he has no learning, I must call him learned.
8. The Master said, A gentleman will not be looked up to unless he is staid, nor will his learning be sound. Put faithfulness and truth first; have no friends unlike thyself; be not ashamed to mend thy faults.
9. Tseng-tzu[5] said, Heed the dead, follow up the past, and the soul of the people will again grow great.
10. Tzu-ch'in[6] said to Tzu-kung,[7] When he comes to a country the Master always hears how it is governed; does he ask, or is it told him?

Tzu-kung said, The Master gets it by his warmth and honesty, by politeness, modesty and yielding. The way the Master asks is unlike other men's asking.

11. The Master said, Whilst thy father lives look for his purpose; when he is gone, look how he walked. To change nothing in thy father's ways for three years may be called pious.
12. Yu-tzu[8] said, To behave with ease is the best part of courtesy. This was the beauty of the old kings' ways; this they followed in small and great. But knowing this, it will not do to give way to ease, unchecked by courtesy. This too is wrong.
13. Yu-tzu said, If pledges are close to right, word can be kept. If attentions are close to courtesy, shame will be kept far. If we do not choose our leaders wrong, we may worship them too.
14. The Master said, A gentleman that does not seek to eat his fill, nor look for ease in his home, who is earnest at work and careful of

---

[4] A disciple
[5] A disciple
[6] A disciple
[7] A disciple
[8] A disciple

speech, who walks with those that keep the Way, and is guided by them, may be said to love learning.

15. Tzu-kung[9] said, Poor, but no flatterer; rich, but not proud: how would that be?

It would do, said the Master; but better still were poor but merry; rich, but loving courtesy.

Tzu-kung said, When the poem says:

If ye cut, if ye file,If ye polish and grind,

is that what is meant?

The Master said, Now I can begin to talk of poetry to Tz'u. Tell him what is gone, and he knows what shall come.

16. The Master said, Not to be known is no sorrow. My sorrow is not knowing men.

---

9 A disciple

Book II

1. The Master said, He that rules by mind is like the north star, steady in his seat, whilst the stars all bend to him.
2. The Master said, The three hundred poems are summed up in the one line, Think no evil.
3. The Master said, Guide the people by law, aline them by punishment; they may shun crime, but they will want shame. Guide them by mind, aline them by courtesy; they will learn shame and grow good.
4. The Master said, At fifteen, I had the will to learn; at thirty, I could stand; at forty, I had no doubts; at fifty, I understood the heavenly Bidding; at sixty, my ears were opened[10]; at seventy, I could do as my heart lusted without trespassing from the square.
5. Meng Yi asked the duty of a son.

    The Master said, Not to transgress.

    As Fan Chi'ih[11] was driving him, the Master said, Meng-sun[12] asked me the duty of a son; I answered, Not to transgress.

    What did ye mean? said Fan Chi'ih.

    To serve our father and mother with courtesy whilst they live; to bury them with courtesy when they die, and to worship them with courtesy.
6. Meng Wu asked the duty of a son.

    The Master said, He should not grieve his father and mother by anything but illness.
7. Tzu-yu[13] asked the duty of a son.

---

[10] Lit., obedient
[11] A disciple
[12] Meng Yi

The Master said, He that can feed his parents is now called a good son. But both dogs and horses are fed, and unless we honour our parents, what is the difference?

8. Tzu-hsia[14] asked the duty of a son.

The Master said, Our manner is the hard part. For the young to be a stay in toil and leave the wine and food to their elders, is this to fulfil their duty?

9. The Master said, If I talk all day to Hui,[15] like a dullard, he never differs from me. But when he is gone, if I watch him when alone, he can carry out what I taught. No, Hui is no dullard!

10. The Master said, See what he does; watch what moves him; search what pleases him: can the man lie hidden? Can the man lie hidden?

11. The Master said, To keep old knowledge warm and get new makes the teacher.

12. The Master said, A gentleman is not a vessel.

13. Tzu-kung[16] asked, What is a gentleman?

The Master said, He puts words into deeds first, and follows these up with words.

14. The Master said, A gentleman is broad and fair; the small man takes sides and is narrow.

15. The Master said, Learning without thought is naught; thought without learning is dangerous.

16. The Master said, To fight strange doctrines does harm.

17. The Master said, Yu,[17] shall I teach thee what is wisdom? To know what we know, and know what we do not know, is wisdom.

18. Tsu-chang[18] learned with an eye to pay.

The Master said, Hear much, leave all that is doubtful alone, speak warily of everything else, and few will be offended. See much, leave all that is dangerous alone, deal warily with everything else, and thou wilt have little to rue. If thy words seldom give offence, and thy deeds leave little to rue, pay will follow.

19. Duke Ai[19] asked, What should I do to win the people?

---

[13] A disciple
[14] A disciple
[15] The disciple Yen Yüan
[16] A disciple
[17] The disciple Tzu-lu
[18] A disciple
[19] Of Lu

Confucius answered, Lift up the straight, put away the crooked; and the people will be won. Lift up the crooked, put away the straight; and the people will not be won.

20. Chi K'ang[20] asked how to make the people lowly, faithful and painstaking.

The Master said, Meet them with dignity, they will be lowly; be a good son and merciful, they will be faithful; lift up the good and teach the unskilled, and they will take pains.

21. One said to Confucius, Why do ye not govern, Sir?

The Master said, What does the Book[21] say of a good son? 'To be a good son and a friend to thy brothers is to show how to govern.' This, too, is to govern. Must one be in office to govern?

22. The Master said, A man without truth, I know not what good he is! A cart without a crosspole, a carriage without a yoke, how can they be moved?

23. Tzu-chang[22] asked whether we can know what is to be ten generations hence.

The Master said, The Yin[23] took over the manners of the Hsia; the harm and the good that they did them can be known. The Chou took over the manners of the Yin; the harm and the good that they did them can be known. And we may know what shall be, even an hundred generations hence, whoever follows Chou.

24. The Master said, To worship the ghosts of men not akin to us is fawning. To see the right and not do it is want of courage.

---

[20] The head of the Chi clan
[21] The Book of History
[22] A disciple
[23] Up to the time of Confucius, China had been ruled by three lines of kings. First the T'ang, next the Yin or Shang, then the Chou

Book III

1. Of the Chi having eight rows of dancers[24] in his courtyard, Confucius said, If this is to be borne, what is not to be borne?
2. When the sacrifice was ended, the Three Clans had the Yung hymn sung.

   The Master said,

   Princes and dukes assist.Solemn is the Son of heaven;

   what meaning has this in the courtyard of the Three Clans?
3. The Master said, A man without love, what is courtesy to him? A man without love, what is music to him?
4. Lin Fang asked what good form is at root.

   The Master said, A big question! At high-tides, thrift is better than waste; at burials, grief is worth more than nicety.
5. The Master said, Every wild tribe has its lord, whereas the lands of Hsia[25] have none!
6. The Chi sacrificed to Mount T'ai.[26]

   The Master said to Jan Yu,[27] Canst thou not stop this?

   He answered, I cannot.

   Alas! said the Master; dost thou think Mount T'ai less wise than Lin Fang?

---

[24] An Imperial prerogative
[25] China
[26] A prerogative of the Duke of Lu
[27] A disciple in the service of the Chi

7. The Master said, A gentleman never strives with others. Or must he, perhaps, in shooting? But then, as he bows and makes way in going up or steps down to drink,[28] his strife is that of a gentleman.

8. Tzu-hsia asked, What is the meaning of:

Her cunning smiles,Her dimples light,Her lovely eyes,So clear and bright,All unadorned,The background white.

Colouring, said the Master, is second to the plain ground.

Then good form is second, said Tzu-hsia.

Shang,[29] said the Master, thou hast hit my meaning! Now I can talk of poetry to thee.

9. The Master said, I can speak of the manners of Hsia; but as proof of them Chi[30] is not enough. I can speak of the manners of Yin; but as proof of them Sung is not enough. This is due to their dearth of books and great men. If there were enough of these, I could use them as proofs.

10. The Master said, After the drink offering at the Great Sacrifice, I have no wish to see more.

11. One asked the meaning of the Great Sacrifice.

The Master said, I do not know. He that knew the meaning would overlook all below heaven as I do this—and he pointed to his palm.

12. He worshipped as if those whom he worshipped were before him; he worshipped the spirits as if they were before him.

The Master said: For me, to take no part in the sacrifice is the same as not sacrificing.

13. Wang-sun Chia[31] said, What is the meaning of, It is better to court the hearth-god than the god of the home?

Not so, said the Master. A sin against Heaven leaves no room for prayer.

14. The Master said, Chou[32] looks back on two lines of kings. How rich, how rich it is in art! I follow Chou.

15. On going into the Great Temple the Master asked about everything.

---

[28] The loser had to drink a cup of wine
[29] Tzu-hsia
[30] Chi was the homeland of the House of Hsia, Sung that of the House of Yin
[31] Wang-sun Chia was minister of Wei, and had more influence than his master. The hearth-god ranks below the god of the home (the Roman lares), but since he sees all that goes on in the house, and ascends to heaven at the end of the year to report what has happened, it is well to be on good terms with him
[32] The royal house of Chou, which was then ruling China

One said, Who says that the Tsou man's son knows the rites? On going into the Great Temple he asked about everything.

When he heard this, the Master said, Such is the rite.

16. The Master said, In shooting, the arrow need not go right through the target, for men are not the same in strength. This was the old rule.
17. Tzu-kung wished to do away with the sheep offering at the new moon.

The Master said, Thou lovest the sheep, Tz'u: I love the rite.

18. The Master said: Serve the king with all courtesy, men call it fawning.
19. Duke Ting asked how a lord should treat his lieges, and how lieges should serve their lord.

Confucius answered, The lord should treat his lieges with courtesy; lieges should serve their lord faithfully.

20. The Master said, The poem *The Osprey* is glad, but not wanton; it is sad, but not morbid.
21. Duke Ai asked Tsai Wo about the earth-altars.

Tsai Wo answered, The Emperors of the house of Hsia grew firs round them; the men of Yin grew cypress; the men of Chou grew chestnut, which was to say, Let the people tremble.[33]

On hearing this, the Master said, I do not speak of what is ended, chide what is settled, or find fault with what is past.[34]

22. The Master said, How shallow was Kuan Chung!

But, said one, was not Kuan Chung thrifty?

The Kuan, said the Master, owned San Kuei, and no one of his household held two posts: was that thrift?

At least Kuan Chung knew good form.

The Master said, Kings screen their gates with trees; the Kuan, too, had trees to screen his gate. When two kings are carousing, they have a stand for the turned-down cups; the Kuan had a turned-down cup-stand, too! If the Kuan knew good form, who does not know good form?[35]

---

[33] Tremble and chestnut have the same sound in Chinese.

[34] In old times men had been sacrificed at the earth-altars, and Tsai Wo's answer might seem to approve the practice

[35] Kuan Chung (+ 645 b.c.), a famous man in his day, was chief minister to the Duke of Ch'i, whom he raised to such wealth and power that he became the leading prince of the empire. His chief merit lay in taming the barbarous frontier tribes. The rest of his work was built upon sand and died with him.

23. The Master said to the Great Master[36] of Lu, We can learn how to play music; at first each part in unison; then a swell of harmony, each part distinct, rolling on to the finish.

24. The warden of Yi asked to see Confucius, saying, No gentleman has ever come here whom I have failed to see.

The followers took him in.

On leaving he said, My two-three boys, why lament your fall? The Way has long been lost below heaven! Now Heaven shall make the Master into a warning bell.

25. The Master said of the music of Shao, It is thoroughly beautiful, and thoroughly good, too. Of the music of Wu, he said, It is thoroughly beautiful, but not thoroughly good.

26. The Master said, Rank without beauty; ceremony without reverence; mourning without grief, why should I cast them a glance?

---

[36] Of music

Book IV

1. The Master said, Love makes a spot beautiful: who chooses not to dwell in love, has he got wisdom?
2. The Master said, Loveless men cannot bear need long, they cannot bear fortune long. Loving men find peace in love, the wise find profit in it.
3. The Master said, Love alone can love others, or hate others.
4. The Master said, A will set on love is free from evil.
5. The Master said, Wealth and honours are what men desire; but do not go from the Way, to keep them. Lowliness and want are hated by men; but do not go from the Way, to escape them.

   Shorn of love, is a gentleman worthy of the name? Not for one moment may a gentleman sin against love; he must not do so in flurry and haste, nor do so in utter overthrow.

6. The Master said, I have seen no one that loves love and hates uncharity. He that loves love will set nothing higher. The hater of uncharity is so given to love that no uncharity can enter into his life. If a man were to give his strength to love for one day, I have seen no one whose strength would fail him. There may be such men, but I have not seen one.
7. The Master said, A man and his faults are of a piece. By watching his faults we learn whether love be his.
8. The Master said, To learn the Way at daybreak and die at eve were enough.
9. The Master said, A knight[37] in quest of the Way, who is ashamed of bad clothes and bad food, it is idle talking to.
10. The Master said, A gentleman has no likes or dislikes below heaven. He follows right.
11. The Master said, The gentleman cherishes mind, the small man cherishes dirt. Gentlemen trust in the law, the small man trusts in favour.

---

[37] Shih: a gentleman entitled to bear arms, not a knight in armour

12. The Master said, The chase of gain is rich in hate.
13. The Master said, What is it to sway a kingdom by courteous yielding? If we cannot sway a kingdom by courteous yielding, what is our courtesy worth?
14. The Master said, Care not for want of place; care for thy readiness to fill one. Care not for being unknown, but seek to be worthy of note.
15. The Master said, One line, Shen,[38] runs through my Way.

Yes, said Tseng-tzu.

After the Master had left, the disciples asked what was meant.

Tseng-tzu said, The Master's Way is no more than faithfulness and fellow-feeling.

16. The Master said, The gentleman is learned in right; the small man is learned in gain.
17. The Master said, At sight of worth, think to grow like it; at sight of baseness, search thyself within.
18. The Master said, A father or a mother may be gently chidden. If thou seest they have no will to follow thee, be the more lowly, but do not give way; nor murmur at the trouble they give thee.
19. The Master said, Whilst thy father and mother are living, do not wander afar. If thou must travel, hold a set course.
20. The Master said, He that changes nothing in his father's ways for three years may be called pious.
21. The Master said, A father and mother's years must be borne in mind; with gladness on the one hand and fear on the other.
22. The Master said, The men of old were loth to speak, for not to live up to their words would have shamed them.
23. The Master said, We shall seldom get lost if we hold to main lines.
24. The Master said, A gentleman wishes to be slow to speak and quick to do.
25. The Master said, A great soul is never friendless: he has always neighbours.
26. Tzu-yu said, Nagging at kings brings disgrace, nagging at friends estrangement.

---

[38] The disciple Tseng-tzu.

Book V

1. Of Kung-yeh Ch'ang the Master said, A girl might be wedded to him. Though he has been in fetters that was not his crime.

   He gave him his daughter to wed.

   Of Nan Jung the Master said, When the land keeps the Way he will not be neglected; and if the land loses the Way he will escape punishment and death.

   He gave him his brother's daughter to wed.

2. Of Tzu-chien[39] the Master said, What a gentleman he is! But if there were no gentlemen in Lu, where could he have picked it up?
3. Tzu-kung asked, And what of me?

   Thou art a vessel, said the Master.

   What kind of vessel?

   A rich temple vessel.

4. One said, Yung[40] has love, but he is not glib.

   The Master said, What is the good of being glib? Fighting men with tongue-craft mostly makes men hate you. Whether love be his I do not know, but what is the good of being glib?

5. The Master moved Ch'i-tiao K'ai to take office.

   He answered, For this I want confidence.

   The Master was pleased.

---

[39] A disciple born in Lu
[40] The disciple Chung-kung

6. The Master said, Forsaken is the Way! I must take ship and stem the seas; and Yu[41] shall go with me.

When Tzu-lu heard this he was glad.

The Master said, Yu loves daring more than I do, but he is at a loss how to take things.

7. Meng Wu asked whether Tzu-lu had love.

I do not know, said the Master.

He asked again.

A land of a thousand chariots might give Yu charge of its levies; but whether love be his I do not know.

And how about Ch'iu?[42]

A town of a thousand households, a clan of an hundred chariots might make Ch'iu governor; but whether love be his I do not know.

And how about Ch'ih?[43]

Standing in the court, girt with his sash, Ch'ih might entertain the guests; but whether love be his I do not know.

8. The Master said to Tzu-kung, Which is the better man, thou or Hui[44]?

He answered, How dare I look as high as Hui? When Hui hears one thing, he understands ten; when I hear one thing I understand two.

The Master said, Thou art not his like. Neither art thou his like, nor am I.

9. Tsai Yü[45] slept in the daytime.

The Master said, Rotten wood cannot be carved, nor are dung walls plastered. Why chide with Yü?

The Master said, When I first met men I listened to their words and took their deeds on trust. When I meet them now, I listen to their words and watch their deeds. I righted this on Yü.

10. The Master said, I have met no firm man.

One answered, Shen Ch'ang.

The Master said, Ch'ang is passionate; how can he be firm?

---

[41] Tzu-lu
[42] The disciple Jan Yu
[43] The disciple Kung-hsi Hua
[44] The disciple Yen Yüan
[45] The disciple Tsai Wo

11. Tzu-kung said, What I do not wish done to me, I likewise wish not to do to others.

   The Master said, That is still beyond thee, Tz'u.

12. Tzu-kung said, To hear the Master on his art and precepts is granted us; but to hear him on man's nature and the Way of Heaven is not.
13. Until Tzu-lu could do what he had heard, his only fear was to hear more.
14. Tzu-kung asked, Why was K'ung-wen called cultured?

   The Master said, He was quick and loved learning; he was not ashamed to ask those beneath him: that is why he was called cultured.

15. The Master said, Of the ways of a gentleman Tzu-ch'an had four. His life was modest; he honoured those that he served. He was kind in feeding the people, and he was just in his calls upon them.
16. The Master said, Yen P'ing was a good friend. The longer he knew you, the more attentive he grew.
17. The Master said, Tsang Wen lodged his tortoise with hills on the pillars and reeds on the uprights: was this his wisdom?
18. Tzu-chang said, The chief minister, Tzu-wen, was thrice made minister without showing gladness, thrice he left office with unmoved looks. He always told the new ministers how the old ones had governed: how was that?

   He was faithful, said the Master.

   But was it love?

   I do not know, said the Master: how should this amount to love?

   When Ts'ui murdered the lord of Ch'i, Ch'en Wen threw up ten teams of horses and left the land. On coming to another kingdom he said, 'Like my lord Ts'ui,' and left it. On coming to a second kingdom he said again, 'Like my lord Ts'ui,' and left it: how was that?

   He was clean, said the Master.

   But was it love?

   I do not know, said the Master: how should this amount to love?

19. Chi Wen thought thrice before acting.

   On hearing this the Master said, Twice is enough.

20. The Master said, Whilst the land kept the Way Ning Wu showed wisdom; when his land lost the Way he grew simple. His wisdom we may come up to; such simplicity is beyond us.[46]

---

[46] Ning Wu was minister of the Duke of Wei in the middle of the seventh century b.c. The duke was driven from his throne and deserted by the wise and prudent;

21. When he was in Ch'en the Master said, Home, I must go home! Zealous, or rash, or finished scholars, my young sons at home do not know what pruning they still need!
22. The Master said, Because Po-yi and Shu-ch'i never remembered old wickedness they made few enemies.[47]
23. The Master said, Who can call Wei-sheng Kao straight? A man begged him for vinegar: he begged it of a neighbour, and gave it.
24. The Master said, Smooth words, fawning looks, and overdone humility, Tso Ch'iu-ming thought shameful, and so do I. He thought it shameful to hide ill-will and ape friendship, and so do I.
25. As Yen Yüan and Chi-lu[48] were sitting with him, the Master said, Why not each of you tell me thy wishes?

Tzu-lu said, I should like carriages and horses, and clothes of light fur to share with my friends, and, if they spoiled them, not to get angry.

Yen Yüan said, I should like to make no boast of talent or show or merit.

Tzu-lu said, We should like to hear your wishes, Sir.

The Master said, To give the old folk peace, to be true to friends, and to have a heart for the young.

26. The Master said, It is finished! I have met no one that can see his own faults and arraign himself within.
27. The Master said, In a hamlet of ten houses there must be men that are as faithful and true men as I, but they do not love learning as I do.

---

but Ning Wu, in his simplicity, stuck to his master and finally effected his restoration

[47] Po-yi and Shu-ch'i were sons of the King of Ku-chu. Their father left the throne to the younger of the two; but he would not supplant the elder, nor would the elder go against his father's wishes. So they both retired into obscurity. When King Wu overthrew the tyrant Chou (1122 b.c.), they starved to death, rather than live under a new dynasty. Of Po-yi Mencius tells us (Book X, chapter 1): 'His eyes would not look on an evil face, his ears would not listen to an evil sound. He served none but his own lord, he ruled none but his own people. He came in when there was order, and withdrew when tumults came. Where lawless rule showed, or lawless people stayed, he could not bear to dwell. To be together with country folk he thought like sitting in court dress and court cap on dust and ashes. In Chou's time he dwelt by the North Sea shore, waiting for all below heaven to grow clean. So, hearing the ways of Po-yi, the fool grows honest, and the weakling's purpose stands.

[48] Tzu-lu

Book VI

1. The Master said, Yung[49] might fill the seat of a prince.

   And might Tzu-sang Po-tzu? asked Chung-kung.

   Yes, said the Master; but he is slack.

   To be stern to himself, said Chung-kung, and slack in his claims on the people, might do; but to be slack himself and slack with others must surely be too slack.

   The Master said, What Yung says is true.

2. Duke Ai asked which disciples loved learning.

   Confucius answered, Yen Hui[50] loved learning. He did not carry over anger; he made no mistake twice. Alas! his mission was short, he died. Now that he is gone, I hear of no one that loves learning.

3. When Tzu-hua[51] was sent to Ch'i, the disciple Jan asked for grain for his mother.

   The Master said, Give her six pecks.

   He asked for more.

   The Master said, Give her sixteen.

   Jan gave her eight hundred.

---

[49] The disciple Chung-kung
[50] The disciple Yen Yüan
[51] The disciple Kung-hsi Hua, or Kung-hsi Ch'ih

The Master said, On his way to Ch'i, Ch'ih[52] was drawn by sleek horses and clad in light furs. I have heard that gentlemen help the needy, not that they swell riches.

When Yüan Ssu was made governor he was given nine hundred measures of grain, which he refused.

Not so, said the Master: why not take it and give it to thy neighbours and countryfolk?

4. The Master said of Chung-kung, If the calf of a brindled cow be red and horned, though men be shy to offer him, will the hills and streams reject him?

5. The Master said, For three months together Hui's[53] heart never sinned against love. The others may hold out for a day, or a month, but no more.

6. Chi K'ang[54] asked whether Chung-yu[55] was fit to govern.

The Master said, Yu[56] is firm; what would governing be to him?

And is Tz'u[57] fit to govern?

Tz'u is thorough; what would governing be to him?

And is Ch'iu[58] fit to govern?

Ch'in is clever; what would governing be to him?

7. The Chi sent to make Min Tzu-ch'ien[59] governor of Pi.

Min Tzu-ch'ien said, Make some good excuse for me. If he sends again I must be across the Wen.

8. When Po-niu[60] was ill the Master asked after him. Grasping his hand through the window, he said, He is going. It is the Bidding; but why this man of such an illness? Why this man of such an illness?

9. The Master said. What a man was Hui![61] A bowl of rice, a gourd of water, in a low alley; man cannot bear such misery! Yet Hui never fell from mirth. What a man he was!

---

[52] Kung-hei Ch'ih
[53] Yen Yüan
[54] The head of the Chi clan after Chi Huan
[55] The disciple Tzu-lu
[56] The disciple Tzu-kung
[57] The disciple Jan Yu.
[58] A disciple
[59] Yen Yüan
[60] Jan Yu
[61] A disciple

10. Jan Ch'iu[62] said, It is not that I take no pleasure in the Master's Way: I want strength.

The Master said, He that wants strength faints midway; but thou drawest a line.

11. The Master said to Tzu-hsia, Study to be a gentleman, not as the small man studies.
12. When Tzu-yu was governor of Wu-ch'eng, the Master said, Hast thou gotten any men?

He answered, I have Tan-t'ai Mieh-ming. He will not take a short cut when walking, and he has never come to my house except on business.

13. The Master said, Meng Chih-fan never brags. He was covering the rear in a rout; but on coming to the gate he whipped his horse and cried, Not courage kept me behind; my horse won't go!
14. The Master said, Unless we are glib as the reader T'o and fair as Chao of Sung, escape is hard in the times that be!
15. The Master said, Who can go out except by the door? Why is it no one keeps to the Way?
16. The Master said, Matter outweighing art begets roughness; art outweighing matter begets pedantry. Matter and art well blent make a gentleman.
17. The Master said, Man is born straight. If he grows crooked and yet lives, he is lucky to escape.
18. The Master said, He that knows is below him that loves, and he that loves below him that delights therein.
19. The Master said, To men above the common we can talk of higher things; to men below the common we must not talk of higher things.
20. Fan Ch'ih[63] asked, What is wisdom?

The Master said, To foster right among the people; to honour ghosts and spirits, and yet keep aloof from them, may be called wisdom.

He asked, What is love?

The Master said, To rank the effort above the prize may be called love.

21. The Master said, Wisdom delights in water; love delights in hills. Wisdom is stirring; love is quiet. Wisdom is merry; love grows old.
22. The Master said, By one revolution Ch'i might grow to be Lu; by one revolution Lu might reach the Way.
23. The Master said, A drinking horn that is no horn! What a horn! What a drinking horn!
24. Tsai Wo[64] said, If a man of love were told that a man is in a well, would he go in after him?

---

[62] A disciple
[63] A disciple.

The Master said, Why should he? A gentleman might be got to the well, but not trapped into it, He may be cheated, but not fooled.

25. The Master said, By breadth of reading and the ties of courtesy, a gentleman is kept, too, from false paths.
26. The Master saw Nan-tzu.[65] Tzu-lu was displeased.

The Master took an oath, saying, If I have done wrong, may Heaven forsake me, may Heaven forsake me!

27. The Master said, The highest minds cleave to the Centre, the Common. They have long been rare among the people.
28. Tzu-kung said, To treat the people with bounty and help the many, how were that? Could it be called love?

The Master said, What has this to do with love? Must it not be holiness? Yao and Shun[66] still yearned for this. Seeking a foothold for self, love finds a foothold for others; seeking light for itself, it enlightens others too. To learn from the near at hand may be called the clue to love.

---

[64] A disciple.
[65] The dissolute wife of Duke Ling of Wei.
[66] Two emperors of the golden age.

Book VII

1. The Master said, A teller and not a maker, one that trusts and loves the past; I might liken myself to our old P'eng.[67]
2. The Master said, To think things over in silence, to learn and be always hungry, to teach and never weary; is any of these mine?
3. The Master said, Not making the most of my mind, want of thoroughness in learning, failure to do the right when told it, lack of strength to overcome faults; these are my sorrows.
4. In his free moments the Master was easy and cheerful.
5. The Master said, How deep is my decay! It is long since I saw the Duke of Chou[68] in a dream.
6. The Master said, Keep thy will on the Way, lean on mind, rest in love, move in art.
7. The Master said, From the man that paid in dried meat upwards, I have withheld teaching from no one.
8. The Master said, Only to those fumbling do I open, only for those stammering do I find the word.

   If I lift one corner and the other three are left unturned, I say no more.

9. When eating beside a mourner the Master never ate his fill. On days when he had been wailing, he did not sing.
10. The Master said to Yen Yüan, To go forward when in office and lie quiet when not; only I and thou can do that.

---

[67] We should be glad to know more of old P'eng, but nothing is known of him
[68] Died 1105 b.c. He was the younger brother of King Wu, the founder of the Chou dynasty, as great in peace as the King in war. He was so bent on carrying out the old principles of government that 'if anything did not tally with them, he looked up and thought, till day passed into night, and if by luck he found the answer he sat and waited for the dawn' (Mencius, Book VIII, chapter 20).

Tzu-lu said, If ye had to lead three armies, Sir, whom would ye have with you?

No man, said the Master, that would face a tiger bare-fisted, or plunge into a river and die without a qualm; but one, indeed, who, fearing what may come, lays his plans well and carries them through.

11. The Master said, If shouldering a whip were a sure road to riches I should turn carter; but since there is no sure road, I tread the path I love.
12. The Master gave heed to abstinence, war and sickness.
13. When he was in Ch'i, for three months after hearing the Shao played, the Master knew not the taste of flesh.

I did not suppose, he said, that music could reach such heights.

14. Jan Yu said, Is the Master for the lord of Wei?[69]

I shall ask him, said Tzu-kung.

He went in, and said, What kind of men were Po-yi[70] and Shu-ch'i?

Worthy men of yore, said the Master.

Did they rue the past?

They sought love and found it; what had they to rue?

Tzu-kung went out, and said, The Master is not for him.

15. The Master said, Eating coarse rice and drinking water, with bent arm for pillow, we may be merry; but ill-gotten wealth and honours are to me a wandering cloud.
16. The Master said, Given a few more years, making fifty for learning the Yi,[71] I might be freed from gross faults.
17. The Master liked to talk of poetry, history, and the upkeep of courtesy. Of all these he liked to talk.
18. The Duke of She asked Tzu-lu about Confucius.

Tzu-lu did not answer.

The Master said, Why didst thou not say, He is a man that forgets to eat in his eagerness, whose sorrows are forgotten in gladness, who knows not that age draws near?

---

[69] The grandson of Duke Ling, the husband of Nan-tzu. His father had been driven from the country for plotting to kill Nan-tzu. When Duke Ling died, he was succeeded by his grandson, who opposed by force his father's attempts to seize the throne
[70] See Book V, § 22
[71] An abstruse, ancient classic, usually called the Book of Changes

19. The Master said, I was not born to wisdom: I loved the past, and sought it earnestly there.
20. The Master never talked of goblins, strength, disorder, or spirits.
21. The Master said, Walking three together I am sure of teachers. I pick out the good and follow it; I see the bad and shun it.
22. The Master said, Heaven begat the mind in me; what can Huan T'ui[72] do to me?
23. The Master said, My two-three boys, do ye think I hide things? I hide nothing from you. I am a man that keeps none of his doings from his two-three boys.
24. The Master taught four things: art, conduct, faithfulness and truth.
25. The Master said, A holy man I shall not live to see; enough could I find a gentleman! A good man I shall not live to see; enough could I find a steadfast one! But when nothing poses as something, cloud as substance and want as riches, it is hard indeed to be steadfast!
26. The Master angled, but he did not fish with a net; he shot, but not at birds sitting.
27. The Master said, There may be men that do things without knowing why. I do not. To hear much, pick out the good and follow it; to see much and think it over; this comes next to wisdom.
28. To talk to the Hu village was hard. When a lad was seen by the Master, the disciples doubted.

The Master said, I allow his coming, not what he does later. Why be so harsh? If a man cleans himself to come in, I admit his cleanness, but do not warrant his past.

29. The Master said, Is love so far a thing? I long for love, and lo! love is come.
30. A judge of Ch'en asked whether Duke Chao[73] knew good form.

Confucius answered, He knew good form.

After Confucius had left, the judge beckoned Wu-ma Ch'i[74] to him, and said, I had heard that gentlemen are of no party, but do they, too, take sides? This lord married a Wu, whose name was the same as his, and called her Miss Tzu of Wu: if he knew good form, who does not know good form?

When Wu-ma Ch'i told the Master this he said, How lucky I am! If I go wrong, men are sure to know it!

---

[72] In 495 b.c., during Confucius's wanderings, Huan T'ui sent a band of men to ·kill him; but why he did so is not known
[73] Duke Chao of Lu (+ 510 b.c.) was the duke that first employed Confucius. It is against Chinese custom for a man to marry a girl whose surname is the same as his
[74] A disciple of Confucius

31. When anyone sang to the Master, and sang well, he made him sing it again and joined in.
32. The Master said, I have no more reading than others; to live as a gentleman is not yet mine.
33. The Master said, How dare I lay claim to holiness or love? A man of endless craving, who never tires of teaching, I might be called, but that is all.

   That is just what we disciples cannot learn, said Kung-hsi Hua.

34. When the Master was very ill, Tzu-lu asked leave to pray.

   Is it done? said the Master.

   It is, answered Tzu-lu. The Memorials say, Pray to the spirits above and to the Earth below.

   The Master said, Long-lasting has my prayer been.

35. The Master said, Waste makes men unruly, thrift makes them mean; but they are better mean than unruly.
36. The Master said, A gentleman is calm and spacious; the small man is always fretting.
37. The Master's manner was warm yet dignified. He was stern, but not fierce; humble, yet easy.

Book VIII

1. The Master said, T'ai-po[75] may be said to have carried nobility furthest. Thrice he refused all below heaven. Men were at a loss how to praise him.
2. The Master said, Without good form attentions grow into fussiness, heed becomes fearfulness, daring becomes unruliness, frankness becomes rudeness. When gentlemen are true to kinsfolk, love will thrive among the people; if they do not forsake old friends, the people will not steal.
3. When Tseng-tzu lay sick he called his disciples and said, Uncover my feet, uncover my arms. The poem says,

   As if a deep gulfWere yawning below,As crossing thin ice,Take heed how ye go.

   My little children, I have known how to keep myself unhurt until now and hereafter.[76]

4. When Tseng-tzu was sick Meng Ching[77] came to ask after him.

   Tseng-tzu said, When a bird is dying his notes are sad; when man is dying his words are good. Three branches of the Way are dear to a gentleman: To banish from his bearing violence and disdain; to sort his

---

[75] T'ai-po was the eldest son of the King of Chou. The father wished his third son to succeed him, so that the throne might pass later to his grandson, afterwards known as King Wen. To enable this plan to be carried out T'ai-po and his second brother went into exile.

[76] The Chinese say: 'The body is born whole by the mother; it should be returned whole by the son.'

[77] Chief of the Meng clan, minister of Lu

face to the truth, and to banish from his speech what is low or unseemly. The ritual of chalice and platter[78] has servitors to see to it.

5. Tseng-tzu said, When we can, to ask those that cannot; when we are more, to ask those that are less; having, to seem wanting; real, to seem shadow; when gainsaid, never answering back; I had a friend[79] once that could do thus.
6. Tseng-tzu said, A man to whom an orphan, a few feet high, or the fate of an hundred towns, may be entrusted, and whom no crisis can corrupt, is he not a gentleman, a gentleman indeed?
7. Tseng-tzu said, The knight had need be strong and bold; for his burden is heavy, the way is far. His burden is love, is it not a heavy one? No halt before death, is that not far?
8. The Master said, Poetry rouses us, we stand upon courtesy, music is our crown.
9. The Master said, The people may be made to follow, we cannot make them understand.
10. The Master said, Love of daring and hatred of poverty lead to crime; a man without love, if he is sorely harassed, turns to crime.
11. The Master said, All the comely gifts of the Duke of Chou,[80] coupled with pride and meanness, would not be worth a glance.
12. The Master said, A man to whom three years of learning have borne no fruit would be hard to find.
13. The Master said, A man of simple faith, who loves learning, who guards and betters his way unto death, will not enter a tottering kingdom, nor stay in a lawless land. When all below heaven follows the Way, he is seen; when it loses the Way, he is unseen. While his land keeps the Way, he is ashamed to be poor and lowly; but when his land has lost the Way, wealth and honours shame him.
14. The Master said, When out of place, discuss not policy.
15. The Master said, In the first days of the music-master Chih how the hubbub[81] of the Kuan-chü rose sea beyond sea! How it filled the ear!
16. The Master said, Of men that are zealous, but not straight; dull, but not simple; helpless, but not truthful, I will know nothing.
17. The Master said, Learn as though the time were short, like one that fears to lose.
18. The Master said, How wonderful were Shun[82] and Yü![83] To have all below heaven was nothing to them!

---

[78] For sacrifice
[79] Probably Yen Yüan
[80] See Book VII, § 5
[81] The last part of the music, when all the instruments were played together
[82] See Introduction
[83] See Introduction

19. The Master said, How great a lord was Yao![84] Wonderful! Heaven alone is great; Yao alone was patterned on it. Vast, boundless! Men's words failed them. The wonder of the work done by him! The flame of his art and precepts!

20. Shun had five ministers, and there was order below heaven.

King Wu[85] said, I have ten uncommon ministers.

Confucius said, 'The dearth of talent,' is not that the truth? When Yü[86] followed T'ang[87] the times were rich in talent; yet there were but nine men in all, and one woman. In greatness of soul we may say that Chou[88] was highest: he had two-thirds of all below heaven and bent it to the service of Yin.

21. The Master said, I see no flaw in Yü. He ate and drank little, yet he was lavish in piety to the ghosts and spirits. His clothes were bad, but in his cap and gown he was fair indeed. His palace buildings were poor, yet he gave his whole strength to dykes and ditches. No kind of flaw can I see in Yü.

---

[84] See Introduction
[85] See Introduction
[86] Shun
[87] Yao
[88] King Wen, Duke of Chou

Book IX

1. The Master seldom spake of gain, or love, or the Bidding.
2. A man of the village of Ta-hsiang said, The great Confucius, with his vast learning, has made no name in anything.

   When the Master heard this, he said to his disciples, What shall I take up? Shall I take up driving, or shall I take up shooting? I shall take up driving.
3. The Master said, A linen cap is good form; now silk is worn. It is cheap, so I follow the many. To bow below is good form; now it is done above. This is arrogance, so, breaking with the many, I still bow below.
4. From four things the Master was quite free: by-ends and 'must' and 'shall' and 'I.'
5. When he was afraid in K'uang,[89] the Master said, Since the death of King Wen, is not the seat of culture here? If Heaven had meant to destroy our culture, a later mortal would have had no part in it. Until Heaven condemns our culture, what can the men of K'uang do to me?
6. A high minister said to Tzu-kung, The Master must be a holy man, he can do so many things!

   Tzu-kung said, Heaven has, indeed, given him so much that he is almost holy, and he can do many things, too.

---

[89] During the Master's wanderings. K'uang is said to have been a small state near Lu which had been oppressed by Yang Huo. Confucius resembled him, and the men of K'uang set upon him, mistaking him for their enemy. The commentators say that the Master was not afraid, only 'roused to a sense of danger.' I cannot find that the text says so.

When the Master heard this, he said, Does the minister know me? Because I was poor when young, I can do many paltry things. But does doing many things make a gentleman? No, not doing many does.

Lao said, The Master would say, As I had no post I learned the crafts.

7. The Master said, Have I in truth wisdom? I have no wisdom. But when a common fellow emptily asks me anything, I tap it on this side and that, and sift it to the bottom.
8. The Master said, The phœnix comes not, the River gives forth no sign: all is over with me!
9. When the Master saw folk clad in mourning, or in cap and gown, or a blind man, he always rose—even for the young,—or, if he was passing them, he quickened his step.
10. Yen Yüan heaved a sigh, and said, As I look up it grows higher, deeper as I dig! I catch sight of it ahead, and on a sudden it is behind me! The Master leads men on, deftly bit by bit. He widens me with culture, he binds me with courtesy. If I wished to stop I could not until my strength were spent. What seems the mark stands near; but though I long to reach it, I find no way.
11. When the Master was very ill, Tzu-lu made the disciples act as ministers.

During a better spell the Master said, Yu has long been feigning. This show of ministers, when I have no ministers, whom will it take in? Will Heaven be taken in? And is it not better to die in the arms of my two-three boys than to die in the arms of ministers? And, if I miss a big burial, shall I die by the roadside?

12. Tzu-kung said, If I had here a fair piece of jade, should I hide it away in a case, or seek a good price and sell it?

Sell it, sell it! said the Master. I tarry for my price.

13. The Master wished to dwell among the nine tribes.[90]

One said, They are low; how could ye?

The Master said, Wherever a gentleman lives, will there be anything low?

14. The Master said. After I came back from Wei to Lu the music was set straight and each song found its place.
15. The Master said, To serve dukes and ministers abroad and father and brothers at home; in matters of mourning not to dare to be slack; and to be no thrall to wine: to which of these have I won?
16. As he stood by a stream, the Master said, Hasting away like this, day and night, without stop!
17. The Master said, I have seen no one that loves mind as he loves looks.

---

[90] In the east of Shantung

18. The Master said, In making a mound, if I stop when one more basket would finish it, I stop. When flattening ground, if, after overturning one basket, I go on, I go ahead.
19. The Master said, Never listless when spoken to, such was Hui.[91]
20. Speaking of Yen Yüan, the Master said, The pity of it! I saw him go on, but I never saw him stop!
21. The Master said, Some sprouts do not blossom, some blossoms bear no fruit!
22. The Master said, Awe is due to youth. May not to-morrow be bright as to-day? To men of forty or fifty, who are still unknown, no awe is due.
23. The Master said, Who would not give ear to a downright word? But to mend is better. Who would not be pleased by a guiding word? But to think it out is better. With such as are pleased but do not think out, or who listen but do not mend, I can do nothing.
24. The Master said, Put faithfulness and truth first; have no friends unlike thyself; be not ashamed to mend thy faults.
25. The Master said, Three armies may be robbed of their leader, no wretch can be robbed of his will.
26. The Master said, Yu[92] is the man to stand, clad in a worn-out quilted gown, unashamed, amid robes of fox and badger!

Without hatred or greed,What but good does he do?

But when Tzu-lu was everlastingly humming these words, the Master said, This is the way towards it, but how much short of goodness itself!

27. The Master said, Erst the cold days show how fir and cypress are last to fade.
28. The Master said, Wisdom has no doubts; love does not fret; the bold have no fears.
29. The Master said, With some we can learn together, but we cannot go their way; we can go the same way with others, though our standpoint is not the same; and with some, though our standpoint is the same our weights and scales are not.

The blossoms of the plum treeAre dancing in play;My thoughts are with thee,In thy home far away.

The Master said, Her thoughts were not with him, or how could he be far away?

---

[91] Yen Yüan
[92] Tzu-lu

Book X

1. Among his own country folk Confucius wore a homely look, like one that has no word to say.

   In the ancestral temple and at court his speech was full, but cautious.

2. At court he talked frankly to men of low rank, winningly to men of high rank. When the king was there, he looked intent and solemn.

3. When the king bade him receive guests, his face seemed to change and his legs to bend. He bowed left and right to those beside him, straightened his robes in front and behind, and swept forward, with arms spread like wings. When the guest had left, he brought back word, saying, The guest is no longer looking.

4. As he went in at the palace gate he stooped, as though it were too low for him. He did not stand in the middle of the gate, or step on the threshold.

   When he passed the throne, his face seemed to change and his legs to bend: he spake with bated breath. As he went up the hall to audience, he lifted his robes, bowed his back, and masked his breathing till it seemed to stop. As he came down, he relaxed his face below the first step and looked pleased. From the foot of the steps he swept forward with arms spread like wings; and when he was back in his seat, he looked intent as before.

5. When he carried the sceptre, his back bent, as under too heavy a burden; he lifted it no higher than in bowing and no lower than in making a gift. His face changed, as it will with fear, and he dragged his feet, as though they were fettered.

   When he offered his present his manner was formal; but at the private audience he was cheerful.

6. The gentleman was never decked in violet or mauve; even at home he would not wear red or purple.

In hot weather he wore an unlined linen gown, but always over other clothes.

With lamb-skin he wore black, with fawn, white, and with fox-skin, yellow. At home he wore a long fur gown, with the right sleeve short.

His nightgown was always half as long again as his body.

In the house he wore thick fur, of fox or badger.

When he was not in mourning there was nothing missing from his girdle.

Except for sacrificial dress, he was sparing of stuff.

He did not wear lamb's fur, or a black cap, on a mourning visit.

At the new moon he always put on court dress and went to court.

7. On his days of abstinence he always wore linen clothes of a pale colour; and he changed his food and moved from his wonted seat.

8. He did not dislike well-cleaned rice or hash chopped small. He did not eat sour or mouldy rice, bad fish, or tainted flesh. He did not eat anything that had a bad colour or that smelt bad, or food that was badly cooked or out of season. Food that was badly cut or served with the wrong sauce he did not eat. However much flesh there might be, it could not conquer his taste for rice. To wine alone he set no limit, but he did not drink enough to muddle him. He did not drink bought wine, or eat ready-dried market meat. He never went without ginger at a meal. He did not eat much.

After a sacrifice at the palace he did not keep the flesh over-night. He never kept sacrificial flesh more than three days. If it had been kept longer it was not eaten.

He did not talk at meals, nor speak when he was in bed.

Even at a meal of coarse rice, or herb broth, or gourds, he made his offering with all reverence.

9. If his mat was not straight, he would not sit down.

10. When the villagers were drinking wine, as those that walked with a staff left, he left too.

At the village exorcisms he put on court dress and stood on the east steps.

11. When sending a man with enquiries to another land, he bowed twice to him and saw him out.

When K'ang gave him some drugs, he bowed, accepted them, and said, I have never taken them; I dare not taste them.

12. On coming back from court after his stables had been burnt, the Master said, Is anyone hurt? He did not ask about the horses.

13. When the king sent him cooked meat, he put his mat straight, and tasted it first; when he sent him raw flesh, he had it cooked, and offered it to the spirits; when he sent him a live beast, he kept it alive.

When he ate in attendance on the king, the king made the offering, he tasted things first.

When he was sick and the king came to see him, he lay with his head to the east, with his court dress over him and his girdle across it.

When he was called by the king's bidding, he walked, without waiting for his carriage.

14. On going into the Great Temple he asked about everything.
15. When a friend died, who had no home to go to, he said, It is for me to bury him.

When friends sent him anything, even a carriage and horses, he never bowed, unless the gift was sacrificial flesh.

16. He did not sleep like a corpse. At home he unbent.

Even if he knew him well, his face changed when he saw a mourner. Even when he was in undress, if he saw anyone in full dress, or a blind man, he looked grave.

To men in deep mourning and to the census-bearers he bowed over the cross-bar.

Before choice meats he rose with changed look. At sharp thunder, or a fierce wind, his look changed.

17. When mounting his carriage he stood straight and grasped the cord. When he was in it, he did not look round, or speak fast, or point.
18. Seeing a man's face, she rose, flew round and settled. The Master said, Hen pheasant on the ridge, it is the season, it is the season.

Tzu-lu went towards her: she sniffed thrice and rose.[93]

---

[93] This passage cannot belong here. It is corrupt and unintelligible

Book XI

1. The Master said, Savages! the men that first went into courtesy and music! Gentlemen! those that went into them later! My use is to follow the first lead in both.
2. The Master said, Not one of my followers in Ch'en or Ts'ai comes any more to my door! Yen Yüan, Min Tzu-ch'ien, Jan Po-niu and Chung-kung were men of noble life; Tsai Wo and Tzu-kung were the talkers; Jan Yu and Chi-lu were statesmen; Tzu-yu and Tzu-hsia, men of arts and learning.
3. The Master said, I get no help from Hui.[94] No word I say but delights him!
4. The Master said, How good a son is Min Tzu-ch'ien! No one finds fault with anything that his father, or his mother, or his brethren say of him.
5. Nan Jung would thrice repeat *The Sceptre White*.[95] Confucius gave him his brother's daughter for wife.
6. Chi K'ang asked which disciples loved learning. Confucius answered, There was Yen Hui[96] loved learning. Alas! his mission was short, he died. Now there is no one.
7. When Yen Yüan died, Yen Lu[97] asked for the Master's carriage to furnish an outer coffin.

   The Master said, Brains or no brains, each of us speaks of his son. When Li[98] died he had an inner but not an outer coffin: I would not go on foot

---

[94] Yen Yüan
[95] The verse runs—
A flaw can be ground
From a sceptre white;
A slip of the tongue
No man can right
[96] Yen Yüan
[97] The father of Yen Yüan
[98] The Master's son

to furnish an outer coffin. As I follow in the wake of the ministers I cannot go on foot.

8. When Yen Yüan died the Master said, Woe is me! Heaven has undone me! Heaven has undone me!

9. When Yen Yüan died the Master gave way to grief.

His followers said, Sir, ye are giving way.

The Master said, Am I giving way? If I did not give way for this man, for whom should I give way to grief?

10. When Yen Yüan died the disciples wished to bury him in pomp.

The Master said, This must not be.

The disciples buried him in pomp.

The Master said, Hui treated me as his father. I have failed to treat him as a son. No, not I; but ye, my two-three boys.

11. Chi-lu[99] asked what is due to the ghosts of the dead?

The Master said, When we cannot do our duty to the living, how can we do it to the dead?

He dared to ask about death.

We know not life, said the Master, how can we know death?

12. Seeing the disciple Min standing at his side with winning looks, Tzu-lu with warlike front, Jan Yu and Tzu-kung frank and free, the Master's heart was glad.

A man like Yu,[100] he said, dies before his day.

13. The men of Lu were building the Long Treasury.

Min Tzu-ch'ien said, Would not the old one do? Why must it be rebuilt?

The Master said, That man does not talk, but when he speaks he hits the mark.

14. The Master said, What has the lute of Yu[101] to do, twanging at my door?

---

[99] Tzu-lu
[100] Tzu-lu. This prophecy came true. Tzu-lu and Tzu-kao were officers of Wei when troubles arose. Tzu-lu hastened to the help of his master. He met Tzu-kao withdrawing from the danger, and was advised to do the same. But Tzu-lu would not desert the man whose pay he drew. He plunged into the fight and was killed
[101] Tzu-lu

But when the disciples looked down on Tzu-lu, the Master said, Yu has come up into hall, but he has not yet entered the inner rooms.

15. Tzu-kung asked, Which is the better, Shih[102] or Shang[103]?

The Master said, Shih goes too far, Shang not far enough.

Then is Shih the better? said Tzu-kung.

Too far, said the Master, is no nearer than not far enough.

16. The Chi was richer than the Duke of Chou; yet Ch'iu[104] became his tax-gatherer and made him still richer.

He is no disciple of mine, said the Master. My little children, ye may beat your drums and make war on him.

17. Ch'ai[105] is simple, Shen[106] is dull, Shih[107] is smooth, Yu[108] is coarse.
18. The Master said, Hui[109] is almost faultless, and he is often empty. Tz'u[110] will not bow to the Bidding, and he heaps up riches; but his views are often sound.
19. Tzu-chang asked, What is the way of a good man?

The Master said, He does not tread the beaten track; and yet he does not enter the inner rooms.

20. The Master said, Commend a man for plain speaking: he may prove a gentleman, or else but seeming honest.
21. Tzu-lu said, Shall I do all I am taught?

The Master said, Whilst thy father and elder brothers live, how canst thou do all thou art taught?

Jan Yu asked, Shall I do all I am taught?

The Master said, Do all thou art taught.

Kung-hsi Hua said, Yu[111] asked, Shall I do all I am taught? and ye said, Sir, Whilst thy father and elder brothers live. Ch'iu[112] asked, Shall I do

---

[102] The disciple Tzu-chang
[103] The disciple Tzu-hsia
[104] The disciple Jan Yu
[105] The disciple Kao Ch'ai
[106] The disciple Tseng-tzu
[107] The disciple Tzu-chang
[108] The disciple Tzu-lu
[109] The disciple Yen Yüan
[110] The disciple Tzu-kung
[111] Tzu-lu
[112] Jan Yu

all I am taught? and ye said, Sir, Do all thou art taught. I am in doubt, and dare to ask you, Sir.

The Master said, Ch'iu is bashful, so I egged him on; Yu is twice a man, so I held him back.

22. When the Master was in fear in K'uang, Yen Yüan fell behind.

The Master said, I held thee for dead.

He answered, Whilst my Master lives how should I dare to die?

23. Chi Tzu-jan[113] asked whether Chung Yu[114] or Jan Ch'iu[115] could be called a great minister.

The Master said, I thought ye would ask me a riddle, Sir, and ye ask about Yu[116] and Ch'iu.[117] He that holds to the Way in serving his lord and leaves when he cannot do so, we call a great minister. Now Yu and Ch'iu I should call tools.

Who are just followers then?

Nor would they follow, said the Master, if told to kill their lord or father.

24. Tzu-lu made Tzu-kao governor of Pi.

The Master said, Thou art undoing a man's son.

Tzu-lu said, What with the people and the spirits of earth and corn, must a man read books to become learned?

The Master said, This is why I hate a glib tongue.

25. The Master said to Tzu-lu, Tseng Hsi,[118] Jan Yu and Kung-hsi Hua as they sat beside him, I may be a day older than you, but forget that. Ye are wont to say, I am unknown. Well, if ye were known, what would ye do?

Tzu-lu answered lightly. Give me a land of a thousand chariots, crushed between great neighbours, overrun by soldiers and searched by famine, and within three years I could put courage into it and high purpose.

The Master smiled.

---

[113] The younger brother of Chi Huan, the head of the Chi clan
[114] Tzu-lu. He and Jan Yu had taken office under the Chi
[115] Jan Yu
[116] Tzu-lu. He and Jan Yu had taken office under the Chi
[117] Jan Yu.
[118] A disciple: the father of Tseng-tzu

What wouldst thou do, Ch'iu[119]? he said.

He answered, Give me a land of sixty or seventy, or fifty or sixty square miles, and within three years I could give the people plenty. As for courtesy and music, they would wait the coming of a gentleman.

And what wouldst thou do, Ch'ih[120]?

He answered, I do not speak of what I can do, but of what I should like to learn. At services in the Ancestral Temple, or at the Grand Audience, I should like to fill a small part.

And what wouldst thou do, Tien[121]?

Tien stopped playing, pushed his still sounding lute aside, rose and answered, My choice would be unlike those of the other three.

What harm in that? said the Master. Each but spake his mind.

In the last days of spring, all clad for the springtime, with five or six young men and six or seven lads, I would bathe in the Yi, be fanned by the wind in the Rain God's glade, and go back home singing.

The Master said with a sigh, I side with Tien.

Tseng Hsi stayed after the other three had left, and said, What did ye think, Sir, of what the three disciples said?

Each but spake his mind, said the Master.

Why did ye smile at Yu,[122] Sir?

Lands are swayed by courtesy, but what he said was not modest. That was why I smiled. Yet did not Ch'iu speak of a state? Where would sixty or seventy, or fifty or sixty, square miles be found that are not a state? And did not Ch'ih too speak of a state? Who but great vassals are there in the Ancestral Temple, or at the Grand Audience? But if Ch'ih were to take a small part, who could fill a big one?

---

[119] Jan Yu
[120] Kung-hsi Hua
[121] Tseng Hsi
[122] Tzu-lu

Book XII

1. Yen Yüan asked, What is love?

    The Master said, Love is to conquer self and turn to courtesy. If we could conquer self and turn to courtesy for one day, all below heaven would turn to love. Does love flow from within, or does it flow from others?

    Yen Yüan said, May I ask what are its signs?

    The Master said, To be always courteous of eye and courteous of ear; to be always courteous in word and courteous in deed.

    Yen Yüan said, Though I am not clever, I hope to live by these words.

2. Chung-kung asked, What is love?

    The Master said, Without the door to behave as though a great guest were come; to treat the people as though we tendered the great sacrifice; not to do unto others what we would not they should do unto us; to breed no wrongs in the state and breed no wrongs in the home.

    Chung-kung said, Though I am not clever, I hope to live by these words.

3. Ssu-ma Niu[123] asked, What is love?

    The Master said, Love is slow to speak.

    To be slow to speak! Can that be called love?

    The Master said, Can that which is hard to do be lightly spoken?

4. Ssu-ma Niu asked, What is a gentleman?

    The Master said, A gentleman knows neither sorrow nor fear.

---

[123] A disciple

No sorrow and no fear! Can that be called a gentleman?

The Master said. He searches his heart: it is blameless; so why should he sorrow, what should he fear?

5. Ssu-ma Niu cried sadly, All men have brothers, I alone have none!

    Tzu-hsia said, I have heard that life and death are allotted, that wealth and honours are in Heaven's hand. A gentleman is careful and does not trip; he is humble towards others and courteous. All within the four seas are brethren; how can a gentleman lament that he has none?

6. Tzu-chang asked, What is insight?

    The Master said, Not to be moved by lap and wash of slander, or by plaints that pierce to the quick, may be called insight. Yea, whom lap and wash of slander, or plaints that pierce to the quick cannot move may be called far-sighted.

7. Tzu-kung asked, What is kingcraft?

    The Master said, Food enough, troops enough, and the trust of the people.

    Tzu-kung said, If it had to be done, which could best be spared of the three?

    Troops, said the Master.

    And if we had to, which could better be spared of the other two?

    Food, said the Master. From of old all men die, but without trust a people cannot stand.

8. Chi Tzu-ch'eng[124] said, It is the stuff alone that makes a gentleman; what can art do for him?

    Alas! my lord, said Tzu-kung, how ye speak of a gentleman! No team overtakes the tongue! The art is no less than the stuff, the stuff is no less than the art. Without the fur, a tiger or a leopard's hide is no better than the hide of a dog or a goat.

9. Duke Ai said to Yu Jo,[125] In this year of dearth I have not enough for my wants; what should be done?

    Ye might tithe the people, answered Yu Jo.

    A fifth is not enough, said the Duke, how could I do with a tenth?

---

[124] Minister of Wei
[125] A disciple of Confucius

When all his folk have enough, answered Yu Jo, shall the lord alone not have enough? When none of his folk have enough, shall the lord alone have enough?

10. Tzu-chang asked how to raise the mind and scatter delusions.

The Master said, Put faithfulness and truth first, and follow the right; the mind will be raised. We wish life to what we love and death to what we hate. To wish it both life and death is a delusion.

Whether prompted by wealth, or not,Yet ye made a distinction.

11. Ching,[126] Duke of Ch'i, asked Confucius, What is kingcraft?

Confucius answered. For the lord to be lord and the liege, liege, the father to be father and the son, son.

True indeed! said the Duke. If the lord were no lord and the liege no liege, the father no father and the son no son, though the grain were there, could I get anything to eat?

12. The Master said, To stint a quarrel with half a word Yu[127] is the man.

Tzu-lu never slept over a promise.

13. The Master said, At hearing lawsuits I am no better than others. What is needed is to stop lawsuits.
14. Tzu-chang asked, What is kingcraft?

The Master said, To be tireless of thought and faithful in doing.

15. The Master said, Breadth of reading and the ties of courtesy will keep us, too, from false paths.
16. The Master said, A gentleman shapes the good in man, he does not shape the bad in him. The small man does the contrary.
17. Chi K'ang[128] asked Confucius how to rule.

Confucius answered, To rule is to set straight. If ye give a straight lead, Sir, who will dare not go straight?

18. Chi K'ang being troubled by robbers asked Confucius about it.

Confucius answered, If ye did not wish it, Sir, though ye rewarded him no man would steal.

---

[126] Confucius was in Ch'i in 517 b.c. The duke was over-shadowed by his ministers and thought of setting aside his eldest son
[127] Tzu-lu

[128] On the death of Chi Huan, his brother Chi K'ang set aside Chi Huan's small son and made himself head of the clan.

19. Chi K'ang, speaking of kingcraft to Confucius, said, To help those that follow the Way, should we kill the men that will not?

Confucius answered, Sir, what need has a ruler to kill? If ye wished for goodness, Sir, the people would be good. The gentleman's mind is the wind, and grass are the minds of small men: as the wind blows, so must the grass bend.

20. Tzu-chang asked, What must a knight be, for him to be called eminent?

The Master said, What dost thou mean by eminence?

Tzu-chang answered, To be famous in the state and famous in his home.

That is fame, not eminence, said the Master. The eminent man is plain and straight, and loves right. He weighs words and scans looks; he takes pains to come down to men. And he shall be eminent in the state and eminent in his house. The famous man wears a mask of love, but his deeds belie it. Self-confident and free from doubts, fame will be his in the state and fame be his in his home.

21. Whilst walking with the Master in the Rain God's glade Fan Ch'ih said to him, May I ask how to raise the mind, amend evil and scatter errors?

Well asked! said the Master. Rank thy work above success, will not the mind be raised? Fight the bad in thee, not the bad in other men, will not evil be mended? One angry morning to forget both self and kin, is that no error?

22. Fan Ch'ih asked, What is love?

The Master said, To love men.

He asked, What is wisdom?

The Master said, To know men.

Fan Ch'ih did not understand.

The Master said, Lift up the straight, put by the crooked, and crooked men will grow straight.

Fan Ch'ih withdrew, and seeing Tzu-hsia, said to him, The Master saw me and I asked him what wisdom is. He answered, Lift up the straight, put by the crooked, and crooked men will grow straight. What did he mean?

How rich a saying! said Tzu-hsia. When Shun[129] had all below heaven he chose Kao-yao from the many, lifted him up, and the men without love

---

[129] An emperor of the golden age

fled. When T'ang[130] had all below heaven, he chose Yi-yin[131] from the many, lifted him up, and the men without love fled.

23. Tzu-kung asked about friends.

The Master said, Talk faithfully to them, and guide them well. If this is no good, stop. Do not bring shame upon thee.

24. Tseng-tzu said, A gentleman gathers friends by culture, and stays love with friendship.

---

[130] The founder of the Shang, or Yin, dynasty
[131] T'ang's chief minister. Yi-yin said, Whomsoever I serve, is he not my lord? Whomsoever I rule, are they not my people? He came in when there was order, and came in too when there were tumults. He said, When Heaven begat the people, the man that first understood was sent to waken those slow to understand, and the man that first woke was sent to waken those slow to wake. I am he that woke first among Heaven's people. With the help of the Way, I shall wake the people! For man or wife, of all the people below heaven, to have missed the blessings of Yao and Shun was the same, he thought, as if he himself had pushed him into the ditch. The burden he shouldered was the weight of all below heaven. (Mencius, Book X, chapter 1.)

44

Book XIII

1. Tzu-lu asked how to rule.

   The Master said, Go before; work hard.

   When asked to say more, he said, Never flag.

2. When he was steward of the Chi, Chung-kung asked how to rule.

   The Master said, Let officers act first; overlook small faults, lift up brains and worth.

   Chung-kung said, How shall I get to know brains and worth to lift them up?

   Lift up those thou dost know, said the Master; and those thou dost not know, will other men pass by?

3. Tzu-lu said, The lord of Wei[132] waits for you, Sir, to govern. How shall ye begin?

   Surely, said the Master, by putting names right.

   Indeed, said Tzu-lu, that is far-fetched, Sir. Why put them right?

   What a savage Yu[133] is! said the Master. A gentleman is tongue-tied when he does not understand. If names are not right, words do not fit. If words do not fit, affairs go wrong. If affairs go wrong, neither courtesy nor music thrive. If courtesy and music do not thrive, law and justice fail. And if law and justice fail them, the people can move neither hand nor foot. So a gentleman must be ready to put names into speech and words into deed. A gentleman is nowise careless of his words.

---

[132] See note to Book VII, § 14. Tzu-lu was his officer
[133] Tzu-lu

4. Fan Ch'ih asked to be taught husbandry.

The Master said. An old husbandman knows more than I do.

He asked to be taught gardening.

The Master said. An old gardener knows more than I do.

After Fan Ch'ih had gone, the Master said, How small a man! If those above love courtesy, no one will dare to slight them; if they love right, no one will dare to disobey; if they love truth, no one will dare to hide the heart. Then, from the four corners of the earth, folk will gather with their children on their backs; and what need will there be for husbandry?

5. The Master said, Though a man have conned three hundred poems, if he stands helpless when put to govern, if he cannot answer for himself when he is sent to the four corners of the earth, many as they are, what have they done for him?
6. The Master said, The man of upright life is obeyed before he speaks; commands even go unheeded when the life is crooked.
7. The Master said, The governments of Lu and Wei are brothers.
8. Speaking of Ching, of the ducal house of Wei, the Master said, He was wise in his private life. When he had begun to save, he said, This seems enough. When he grew better off, he said, This seems plenty. When he had grown rich, he said. This seems splendour.
9. When Jan Yu was driving him to Wei, the Master said. What numbers!

Jan Yu said, Since numbers are here, what next is needed?

Wealth, said the Master.

And what comes next after wealth?

Teaching, said the Master.

10. The Master said, If I were employed for a twelve-month, much could be done. In three years all would be ended.
11. The Master said, If good men were to govern a land for an hundred years, cruelty would be conquered and putting to death done away with. How true are these words!
12. The Master said, Even if a king were to govern, a lifetime would pass before love dawned!
13. The Master said, What is governing to a man that can rule himself? If he cannot rule himself, how shall he rule others?
14. As the disciple Jan[134] came back from court, the Master said to him. Why so late?

I had business of state, he answered.

---

[134] Jan Yu. He was in the service of the Chi, not of the Duke of Lu.

Household business, said the Master. If it had been business of state, though I am out of office, I should have heard of it.

15. Duke Ting asked, Is there any one saying that can bless a kingdom?

Confucius answered, That is more than words can do. But men have a saying, To be lord is hard and to be minister is not easy. And if one knew how hard it is to be lord, might not this one saying almost bless a kingdom?

And is there any one saying that can wreck a kingdom?

That is more than words can do, Confucius answered. But men have a saying, My only delight in being lord is that no one withstands what I say. Now if what he says is good, and no one withstands him, is not that good too? But if it is not good, and no one withstands him, might not this one saying almost wreck a kingdom?

16. The Duke of She asked, What is kingcraft?

The Master answered, For those near us to be happy and those far off to come.

17. When he was governor of Chü-fu, Tzu-hsia asked how to rule.

The Master said, Be not eager for haste; look not for small gains. Nothing done in haste is thorough, and looking for small gains big things are left undone.

18. The Duke of She told Confucius, Among the upright men of my clan if the father steals a sheep his son bears witness.

Confucius answered, Our clan's uprightness is unlike that. The father screens his son and the son screens his father. There is uprightness in this.

19. Fan Ch'ih asked, What is love?

The Master said, To be humble at home, earnest at work, and faithful to all. Even among wild tribes none of this must be dropped.

20. Tzu-kung asked, What is it that we call knighthood?

The Master said, To be called a knight, a man must be shamefast in all that he does, if he is sent to the four corners of the earth he must not disgrace his lord's commands.

May I ask who would come next?

He that his clansmen call a good son and his neighbours call modest.

And who would come next?

A man that clings to his word and sticks to his course, a flinty little fellow, would perhaps come next.

And how are the crown servants of to-day?

What! The weights and measures men! said the Master. Are they worth reckoning?

21. The Master said, As I cannot get men of the middle way I have to fall back on zealous and austere men. Zealous men push ahead and take things up, and there are things that austere men will not do.
22. The Master said, The men of the south have a saying, 'Unless he is stable a man will make neither a wizard nor a leech.' This is true. 'His instability of mind may disgrace him.'

The Master said, Neglect of the omens, that is all.

23. The Master said, Gentlemen unite, but are not the same. Small men are all the same, but each for himself.
24. Tzu-kung said, If the whole countryside loved a man, how would that be?

It would not do, said the Master.

And how would it be, if the whole countryside hated him?

It would not do, said the Master. It would be better if all the good men of the countryside loved him and all the bad men hated him.

25. The Master said, A gentleman is easy to serve and hard to please. If we go from the Way to please him, he is not pleased; but his commands are measured to the man. A small man is hard to serve and easy to please. Though we go from the Way to please him, he is pleased; but he expects everything of his men.
26. The Master said, A gentleman is high-minded, not proud; the small man is proud, but not high-minded.
27. The Master said, Strength and courage, simplicity and modesty are akin to love.
28. Tzu-lu asked, When can a man be called a knight?

The Master said, To be earnest, encouraging and kind may be called knighthood: earnest and encouraging with his friends, and kind to his brothers.

29. The Master said, If a good man taught the people for seven years, they would be fit to bear arms too.
30. The Master said, To take untaught men to war is called throwing them away.

Book XIV

1. Hsien[135] asked, What is shame?

   The Master said, To draw pay when the land keeps the Way and to draw pay when it has lost the Way, is shame.

2. To eschew strife and bragging, spite and greed, would that be love?

   The Master said, That may be hard to do; but I do not know that it is love.

3. The Master said, A knight that is fond of ease does not amount to a knight.

4. The Master said, Whilst the land keeps the Way, be fearless of speech and fearless in deed; when the land has lost the Way, be fearless in deed but soft of speech.

5. The Master said, A man of mind can always talk, but talkers are not always men of mind. Love is always bold, though boldness is found without love.

6. Nan-kung Kuo said to Confucius, Yi[136] shot well, Ao pushed a boat over land: each died before his time. Yü and Chi toiled at their crops, and had all below heaven.

   The Master did not answer. But when Nan-kung Kuo had gone, he said, What a gentleman he is! How he honours mind!

7. The Master said, Alas! there have been gentlemen without love! But there has never been a small man that was not wanting in love.

8. The Master said, Can he love thee that never tasks thee? Can he be faithful that never chides?

---

135 The disciple Yüan Ssu
136 Yi was killed by his best pupil, who said to himself, In all the world no one but Yi shoots better than I do. So he killed him

9. The Master said, The decrees were drafted by P'i Shen, criticised by Shih-shu, polished by the Foreign Minister Tzu-yü, and given the final touches by Tzu-ch'an of Tung-li.

10. When he was asked what he thought of Tzu-ch'an, the Master said, A kind-hearted man.

Asked what he thought of Tzu-hsi, the Master said, Of him! What I think of him!

Asked what he thought of Kuan Chung,[137] the Master said, He was the man that drove the Po from the town of Pien with its three hundred households to end his days on coarse rice, without his muttering a word.

11. The Master said, Not to grumble at being poor is hard, not to be proud of wealth is easy.

12. The Master said, Meng Kung-ch'o is more than fit to be steward of Chao or Wei, but he could not be minister of T'eng or Hsieh.

13. Tzu-lu asked what would make a full-grown man.

The Master said, The wisdom of Tsang Wu-chung, Kung-ch'o's lack of greed, Chuang of Pien's boldness and the skill of Jan Ch'iu, graced by courtesy and music, might make a full-grown man.

But now, he said, who asks the like of a full-grown man? He that in sight of gain thinks of right, who when danger looms stakes his life, who, though the bond be old, does not forget what he has been saying all his life, might make a full-grown man.

14. Speaking of Kung-shu Wen, the Master said to Kung-ming Chia, Is it true that thy master does not speak, nor laugh, nor take a gift?

Kung-ming Chia answered, That is saying too much. My master only speaks when the time comes, so no one tires of his speaking; he only laughs when he is merry, so no one tires of his laughter; he only takes when it is right to take, so no one tires of his taking.

It may be so, said the Master; but is it?

15. The Master said, When he held Fang and asked Lu to appoint an heir, though Tsang Wu-chung said he was not forcing his lord, I do not believe it.

16. The Master said, Duke Wen of Chin was deep, but dishonest; Duke Huan of Ch'i was honest, but shallow.

17. Tzu-lu said, When Duke Huan slew the young duke Chiu, and Shao Hu died with him, but Kuan Chung did not, was not this want of love?[138]

---

[137] See note to Book III, § 22
[138] Chiu and Huan were brothers, sons of the Duke of Ch'i. When their father died, their uncle seized the throne. To preserve the rightful heir, Shao Hu and

The Master said, Duke Huan gathered the great vassals round him, not by chariots of war, but through the might of Kuan Chung. What can love do more? What can love do more?

18. Tzu-kung said, When Duke Huan slew the young duke Chiu, and Kuan Chung could not face death and even became his minister, surely he showed want of love?

The Master said, By Kuan Chung helping Duke Huan to put down the great vassals and make all below heaven one, men have fared the better from that day to this. But for Kuan Chung our hair would hang down our backs and our coats would button to the left; or should he, like the bumpkin and his lass, their troth to keep, have drowned in a ditch, unknown to anyone?

19. The minister Hsien, who had been steward to Kung-shu Wen, went to audience of the Duke together with Wen.

When the Master heard of it, he said, He is rightly called Wen (well-bred).

20. The Master spake of Ling Duke of Wei's contempt for the Way.

K'ang[139] said, If this be so, how does he escape ruin?

Confucius answered, With Chung-shu Yü in charge of the guests, the reader T'o in charge of the Ancestral Temple, and Wang-sun Chia in charge of the troops, how should he come to ruin?

21. The Master said, When words are unblushing, they are hard to make good.
22. Ch'en Ch'eng murdered Duke Chien.[140]

Confucius bathed, and went to court and told Duke Ai, saying, Ch'en Heng has murdered his lord: pray, punish him.

The Duke said, Tell the three chiefs.

Kuan Chung fled with Chiu to Lu, whilst Huan escaped to another state. Later on the usurper was murdered, and Huan returned to Ch'i and secured the throne. He then required the Duke of Lu to kill his brother and deliver up to him Shao Hu and Kuan Chung. This was done. But on the way to Ch'i Shao Hu killed himself. Kuan Chung, on the other hand, took service under Duke Huan, became his chief minister, and raised the state to greatness. (See note to Book III, § 22.)
[139] Chi K'ang

[140] 481 b.c., two years before the death of Confucius, who was not at the time in office. Chien was Duke of Ch'i, a state bordering on Lu. The three chiefs were the heads of the three great clans that were all-powerful in Lu.

Confucius said, As I follow in the wake of the ministers, I dared not leave this untold; but the lord says, Tell the three chiefs.

He told the three chiefs. It did no good.

Confucius said, As I follow in the wake of the ministers, I dared not leave this untold.

23. Tzu-lu asked how to serve a lord.

The Master said, Never cheat him; stand up to him.

24. The Master said, A gentleman's life leads upwards; the small man's life leads down.
25. The Master said, The men of old learned for their own sake; to-day men learn for show.
26. Ch'ü Po-yü sent a man to Confucius.

As they sat together, Confucius asked him, What does your master do?

He answered, My master wishes to make his faults fewer, but cannot.

When the messenger had left, the Master said, A messenger, a messenger indeed!

27. The Master said, When not in office discuss not policy.
28. Tseng-tzu said, Even in his thoughts, a gentleman does not outstep his place.
29. The Master said, A gentleman is shamefast of speech: his deeds go further.
30. The Master said, In the way of the gentleman there are three things that I cannot achieve. Love is never troubled; wisdom has no doubts; courage is without fear.

That is what ye say, Sir, said Tzu-kung.

31. Tzu-kung would liken this man to that.

The Master said, What talents Tz'u has! Now I have no time for this.

32. The Master said, Sorrow not at being unknown; sorrow for thine own shortcomings.
33. The Master said, Not to expect to be cheated, nor to look for falsehood, and yet to see them coming, shows worth in a man.
34. Wei-sheng Mou said to Confucius, How dost thou still find roosts to roost on, Ch'iu, unless by wagging a glib tongue?

Confucius answered, I dare not wag a glib tongue; but I hate stubbornness.

35. The Master said, A steed is not praised for his strength, but praised for his mettle.
36. One said, To mete out good for evil, how were that?

And how would ye meet good? said the Master. Meet evil with justice; meet good with good.

37. The Master said, Alas! no man knows me! Tzu-kung said, Why do ye say, Sir, that no man knows you?

The Master said, Never murmuring against Heaven, nor finding fault with men; learning from the lowest, cleaving the heights. I am known but to one, but to Heaven.

38. Liao, the duke's uncle, spake ill of Tzu-lu to Chi-sun.[141]

Tzu-fu Ching-po told this to Confucius, saying, My master's mind is surely being led astray by the duke's uncle, but I have still the strength to expose his body in the market-place.

The Master said, If the Way is to be kept, that is the Bidding, and if the Way is to be lost, this is the Bidding. What can the duke's uncle do against the Bidding?

39. The Master said, Men of worth flee the world; the next best flee the land. Then come those that go at a look, then those that go at words.
40. The Master said, Seven men did so.
41. Tzu-lu spent a night at Shih-men.

The gate-keeper asked him, Whence comest thou?

From Confucius, answered Tzu-lu.

The man that knows it is no good and yet must still be doing? said the gate-keeper.

42. When the Master was chiming his sounding stones in Wei, a basket-bearer said, as he passed the door, The heart is full that chimes those stones! But then he said, For shame! What a tinkling sound! If no one knows thee, have done!

Wade the deep places,Lift thy robe through the shallows!

The Master said, Where there's a will, that is nowise hard.

43. Tzu-chang said, What does the Book mean by saying that Kao-tsung[142] in his mourning shed did not speak for three years?

Why pick out Kao-tsung? said the Master. The men of old were all thus. For three years after their lord had died, the hundred officers did each his duty and hearkened to the chief minister.

---

[141] The head of the Chi clan, in whose service Tzu-lu was
[142] An emperor of the Yin dynasty

44. The Master said, When those above love courtesy, the people are easy to lead.

45. Tzu-lu asked, What makes a gentleman?

    The Master said, To be bent on becoming better.

    Is that all? said Tzu-lu.

    By becoming better to bring peace to men.

    And is that all?

    By becoming better to bring peace to all men, said the Master. Even Yao and Shun were still struggling to become better, and so bring peace to all men.

46. Yüan Jang awaited the Master squatting.

    Unruly when young, unmentioned as man, undying when old, spells good-for-nothing! said the Master, and he hit him on the leg with his staff.

47. When a lad from the village of Ch'üeh was made messenger, someone asked, saying, Is it because he is doing well?

    The Master said, I have seen him sitting in a man's seat, and seen him walking abreast of his elders. He does not try to do well: he wishes to be quickly grown up.

Book XV

1. Ling, Duke of Wei, asked Confucius about the line of battle.

   Confucius answered. Of the ritual of dish and platter[143] I have heard somewhat: I have not learnt warfare.

   He left the next day.

   In Ch'en grain ran out. His followers were too ill to rise. Tzu-lu showed that he was put out.

   Has a gentleman to face want too? he said.

   Gentlemen have indeed to face want, said the Master. The small man, when he is in want, runs to excess.

2. The Master said, Tz'u,[144] dost thou not take me for a man that has learnt much and thought it over?

   Yes, he answered: is it not so?

   No, said the Master. I string all into one.

3. The Master said, Yu,[145] how few men know great-heartedness!
4. The Master said, To rule doing nothing, was what Shun did. For what is there to do? Self-respect and to set the face to rule, is all.
5. Tzu-chang asked how to get on.

   The Master said, Be faithful and true of word, plain and lowly in thy walk; thou wilt get on even in tribal lands. If thy words be not faithful and true, thy walk not plain and lowly, wilt thou get on even in thine own

---

[143] For sacrifice
[144] Tzu-kung
[145] Tzu-lu: probably said to him on the occasion mentioned in § I

town? Standing, see these words ranged before thee; driving, see them written upon the yoke. Then thou wilt get on.

Tzu-chang wrote them on his girdle.

6. The Master said, Straight indeed was the historian Yü! Like an arrow whilst the land kept the Way; and like an arrow when it lost the Way! What a gentleman was Ch'ü Po-yü! Whilst the land kept the Way he took office, and when the land had lost the Way he rolled himself up in thought.
7. The Master said, Not to speak to him that has ears to hear is to spill the man. To speak to a man without ears to hear is to spill thy words. Wisdom spills neither man nor words.
8. The Master said, A high will, or a loving heart, will not seek life at cost of love. To fulfil love they will kill the body.
9. Tzu-kung asked how to attain to love.

The Master said, A workman bent on good work must first sharpen his tools. In the land that is thy home, serve those that are worthy among the great and make friends with loving knights.

10. Yen Yüan asked how to rule a kingdom.

The Master said, Follow the Hsia seasons, drive in the chariot of Yin, wear the head-dress of Chou, take for music the Shao and its dance. Banish the strains of Cheng and flee men that are glib; for the strains of Cheng are wanton and glib speakers are dangerous.

11. The Master said. Without thought for far off things, there shall be trouble near at hand.
12. The Master said, All is ended! I have seen no one that loves mind as he loves looks!
13. The Master said, Did not Tsang Wen filch his post? He knew the worth of Liu-hsia Hui,[146] and did not stand by him.
14. The Master said, By asking much of self and little of other men ill feeling is banished.
15. The Master said, Unless a man say, Would this do? Would that do? I can do nothing for him.

---

[146] Another of these seigneurs du temps jadis that is more to us than a dim shadow, for he still lives in the pages of Mencius, who tells us that, He was not ashamed of a foul lord, and did not refuse a small post. On coming in he did not hide his worth, but held his own way. Neglected and idle, he did not grumble; straitened and poor, he did not mope. When brought together with country folk he was quite at his ease and could not bear to leave them. Thou art thou, he said, and I am I: standing beside me with thy coat off, or thy body naked, how canst thou defile me? (Book X, chapter 1). He stopped if a hand was raised to stop him, for he did not care whether he went or no (Book III, chapter 9)

16. The Master said, When all day long there is no talk of right, and little wiles find favour, the company is in hard case.
17. The Master said, Right is the stuff of which a gentleman is made. Done with courtesy, spoken with humility, rounded with truth, right makes a gentleman.
18. The Master said, His shortcomings trouble a gentleman; to be unknown does not trouble him.
19. The Master said, A gentleman fears that his name shall be no more heard when life is done.
20. The Master said, A gentleman asks of himself, the small man asks of others.
21. The Master said, A gentleman is firm, not quarrelsome; a friend, not a partisan.
22. The Master said, A gentleman does not raise a man for his words, nor spurn the speech for the man.
23. Tzu-kung said, Is there one word by which we may walk till life ends?

The Master said, Fellow-feeling, perhaps. Do not do unto others what thou wouldst not have done to thee.

24. The Master said, Of the men that I meet, whom do I cry down, whom do I overpraise? Or, if I overpraise them, it is after testing them. It was owing to this people that the three lines of kings went the straight way.
25. The Master said, I have still known historians that would leave a gap in their text, and men that would lend a horse to another to ride. Now it is so no more.
26. The Master said, Cunning words confound the mind; petty impatience confounds great projects.
27. The Master said, The hatred of the many must be looked into; the love of the many must be looked into.
28. The Master said, The man can exalt the Way: it is not the Way that exalts the man.
29. The Master said, The fault is to cleave to a fault.
30. The Master said, I have spent whole days without food and whole nights without sleep, thinking, and gained nothing by it. Learning is better.
31. The Master said, A gentleman thinks of the Way; he does not think of food. Sow, and famine may follow; learn, and pay may come; but a gentleman grieves for the Way; to be poor does not grieve him.
32. The Master said, What wisdom has got will be lost again, unless love hold it fast. Wisdom to get and love to hold fast, without dignity of bearing, will not be honoured among men. Wisdom to get, love to hold fast and dignity of bearing, without courteous ways are not enough.
33. The Master said, A gentleman has no small knowledge, but he can carry out big things: the small man can carry out nothing big, but he may be knowing in small things.
34. The Master said, Love is more to the people than fire and water. I have seen men come to their death by fire and water: I have seen no man that love brought to his death.
35. The Master said, When love is at stake yield not to an army.

36. The Master said, A gentleman is consistent, not changeless.
37. The Master said, A servant of the king honours his work, and puts food after it.
38. The Master said, Learning knows no rank.
39. The Master said, Mingle not in projects with a man whose way is not thine.
40. The Master said, The whole end of speech is to be understood.
41. When he saw the music-master Mien, the Master said, as they came to the steps, Here are the steps. On coming to the mat, he said, Here is the mat. When all were seated, the Master told him, He and he are here.

After the music-master had gone, Tzu-chang said, Is this the way to speak to a music-master?

The Master said, Surely it is the way to help a music-master.[147]

---

[147] The man being blind, as so many musicians are in the East

Book XVI

1. The Chi was about to make war on Chuan-yü.[148]

    When Confucius saw Jan Yu and Chi-lu,[149] they said to him, The Chi is going to deal with Chuan-yü.

    Confucius said, After all, Ch'iu,[150] art thou not in the wrong? The kings of old made Chuan-yü lord of Tung Meng.[151] Moreover, as Chuan-yü is inside our borders it is the liege of the spirits of earth and corn of our land; so how can ye make war upon it?

    Jan Yu said, Our master wishes it. Tzu-lu and I, his two ministers, do not, either of us, wish it.

    Confucius said, Ch'iu, Chou Jen used to say, 'He that can put forth his strength takes his place in the line; he that cannot stands back.' Who would take to help him a man that is no stay in danger and no support in falling? Moreover, what thou sayest is wrong. If a tiger or a buffalo escapes from his pen, if tortoiseshell or jade is broken in its case, who is to blame?

    Jan Yu said, But Chuan-yü is now strong, and it is near to Pi[152]; if it is not taken now, in days to come it will bring sorrow on our sons and grandsons.

---

[148] A small feudatory state of Lu

[149] Tzu-lu. He and Jan Yu were in the service of the Chi

[150] Jan Yu

[151] A mountain in Chuan-yü. Since the Emperor had given the ruler of Chuan-yü the right to sacrifice to its mountains, that state had some measure of independence, though it was feudatory to Lu, and within its borders

[152] A town belonging to the Chi

Ch'iu, said Confucius, instead of saying 'I want it,' a gentleman hates to plead that he needs must. I have heard that fewness of men does not vex a king or a chief, but unlikeness of lot vexes him. Poverty does not vex him, but want of peace vexes him. For if wealth were even, no one would be poor. In harmony is number; peace prevents a fall. Thus, if far off tribes will not submit, bring them in by encouraging mind and art, and when they come in give them peace. But now, when far off tribes will not submit, ye two, helpers of your lord, cannot bring them in. The kingdom is split and falling, and ye cannot save it. Yet inside our land ye plot to move spear and shield! The sorrows of Chi's grandsons will not rise in Chuan-yü, I fear: they will rise within the palace wall.

2. Confucius said, When the Way is kept below heaven, courtesy, music and punitive wars flow from the Son of heaven. When the Way is lost below heaven, courtesy, music and punitive wars flow from the great vassals. When they flow from the great vassals they will rarely last for ten generations. When they flow from the great ministers they will rarely last for five generations. When underlings sway the country's fate they will rarely last for three generations. When the Way is kept below heaven power does not lie with the great ministers. When the Way is kept below heaven common folk do not argue.

3. Confucius said, For five generations its income has passed from the ducal house;[153] for four generations power has lain with the great ministers: and humbled, therefore, are the sons and grandsons of the three Huan.

4. Confucius said, There are three friends that help us, and three that do us harm. The friends that help us are a straight friend, an outspoken friend, and a friend that has heard much. The friends that harm us are plausible friends, friends that like to flatter, and friends with a glib tongue.

5. Confucius said, There are three delights that do good, and three that do us harm. Those that do good are delight in dissecting good form and music, delight in speaking of the good in men, and delight in having many worthy friends. Those that do harm are proud delights, delight in idle roving, and delight in the joys of the feast.

6. Confucius said. Men that wait upon lords fall into three mistakes. To speak before the time has come is rashness. Not to speak when the time has come is secrecy. To speak heedless of looks is blindness.

7. Confucius said, A gentleman has three things to guard against.

In the days of thy youth, ere thy strength is steady, beware of lust. When manhood is reached, in the fulness of strength, beware of strife. In old age, when thy strength is broken, beware of greed.

---

[153] Of Lu

8. Confucius said, A gentleman holds three things in awe. He is in awe of the Bidding of Heaven; he is in awe of great men; and he is awed by the words of the holy.

The small man knows not the Bidding of Heaven, and holds it not in awe. He is saucy towards the great; he makes game of holy men's words.

9. Confucius said, The best men are born wise. Next come those that grow wise by learning; then those that learn from toil. Those that do not learn from toil are the lowest of the people.
10. Confucius said, A gentleman has nine aims. To see clearly; to understand what he hears; to be warm in manner, dignified in bearing, faithful of speech, keen at work; to ask when in doubt; in anger to think of difficulties; and in sight of gain to think of right.
11. Confucius said, In sight of good to be filled with longing; to look on evil as scalding to the touch: I have seen such men, I have heard such words.

To live apart and search thy will; to achieve thy Way, by doing right: I have heard these words, but I have seen no such men.

12. Ching, Duke of Ch'i, had a thousand teams of horses; but the people, on his death day, found no good in him to praise. Po-yi[154] and Shu-ch'i[155] starved at the foot of Shou-yang, and to this day the people still praise them.

Is not this the clue to that?

13. Ch'en K'ang[156] asked Po-yü,[157] Apart from us, have ye heard anything, Sir?

He answered, No: once as my father stood alone and I sped across the hall, he said to me, Art thou learning poetry? I answered, No. He that does not learn poetry, he said, has no hold on words. I withdrew and learned poetry.

Another day, when he again stood alone and I sped across the hall, he said to me, Art thou learning courtesy? I answered, No. He that does not learn courtesy, he said, has no foothold. I withdrew and learned courtesy. These two things I have heard.

Ch'en K'ang withdrew, and cried gladly, I asked one thing, and I get three! I hear of poetry; I hear of courtesy; and I hear too that a gentleman stands aloof from his son.

---

[154] See note to Book V, § 22
[155] See note to Book V, § 22
[156] The disciple Tzu-ch'in
[157] The son of Confucius

14. A king speaks of his wife as 'my wife.' She calls herself 'handmaid.' Her subjects speak of her as 'our lord's wife,' but when they speak to foreigners, they say 'our little queen.' Foreigners speak of her, too, as 'the lord's wife.'

Book XVII

1. Yang Huo[158] wished to see Confucius. Confucius did not go to see him. He sent Confucius a sucking pig. Confucius chose a time when he was out, and went to thank him. They met on the road.

    He said to Confucius, Come, let us speak together. To cherish a gem, and undo the kingdom, can that be called love?

    It cannot, said Confucius.

    To love office, and miss the hour again and again, can that be called wisdom?

    It cannot, said Confucius.

    The days and months go by; the years do not wait for us.

    True, said Confucius; I must take office.

2. The Master said, Men are near to each other by nature; the lives they lead sunder them.
3. The Master said, Only the wisest and stupidest of men never change.
4. As the Master came to Wu-ch'eng[159] he heard sounds of lute and song.

    Why use an ox-knife to kill a fowl? said the Master, with a pleased smile.

    Tzu-yu answered, Master, once I heard you say, A gentleman that has learnt the Way loves men; small folk that have learnt the Way are easy to rule.

    My two-three boys, said the Master, what Yen[160] says is true. I spake before in play.

---

158 The all-powerful, unscrupulous minister of the Chi
159 A very small town, of which the disciple Tzu-yu was governor

5. Kung-shan Fu-jao[161] held Pi in rebellion. He called the Master, who wished to go.

Tzu-lu said in displeasure. This cannot be! why must ye go to Kung-shan?

The Master said, He calls me, and would that be all? Could I not make an Eastern Chou[162] of him that uses me?

6. Tzu-chang asked Confucius what is love.

Confucius said, Love is to mete out five things to all below heaven.

May I ask what they are?

Modesty and bounty, said Confucius, truth, earnestness and kindness. Modesty escapes insult: bounty wins the many; truth gains men's trust; earnestness brings success; and kindness is enough to make men work.

7. Pi Hsi called the Master, who wished to go.

Tzu-lu said, Master, I heard you say once, To men whose own life is evil, no gentleman will go. Pi Hsi holds Chung-mou in rebellion; how could ye go to him, Sir?

Yes, I said so, answered the Master. But is not a thing called hard that cannot be ground thin; white, if steeping will not turn it black? And am I a gourd? Can I hang without eating?

8. The Master said, Hast thou heard the six words, Yu,[163] and the six they sink into?

He answered. No.

Sit down, and I shall tell thee. The thirst for love, without love of learning, sinks into simpleness. Love of knowledge, without love of learning, sinks into vanity. Love of truth, without love of learning, sinks into cruelty. Love of straightness, without love of learning, sinks into rudeness. Love of daring, without love of learning, sinks into turbulence. Love of strength, without love of learning, sinks into oddity.

9. The Master said, My little children, why do ye not learn poetry? Poetry would ripen you; teach you insight, friendliness and forbearance; show you how to serve your father at home; and teach your lord abroad; and it would teach you the names of many birds and beasts, plants and trees.

---

[160] Tzu-yu
[161] Steward of the Chi, and a confederate of Yang Huo
[162] A kingdom in the east to match Chou in the west, the home of Kings Wen and Wu
[163] Tzu-lu

10. The Master said to Po-yü,[164] Hast thou done the Chou-nan and Shao-nan?[165] He that has not done the Chou-nan and Shao-nan is like a man standing with his face to the wall.

11. The Master said, 'Courtesy, courtesy,' is the cry; but are jade and silk the whole of courtesy? 'Music, music,' is the cry; but are bells and drums the whole of music?

12. The Master said, Fierce looks and weakness within are like the small man, like the thief that breaks through or clambers over a wall.

13. The Master said, The plain townsman is the bane of mind.

14. The Master said, To tell unto the dust all that we hear upon the way is to lay waste the mind.

15. The Master said, How can we serve the king with a low fellow, who is itching to get what he wants and trembling to lose what he has? This trembling to lose what he has may lead him anywhere.

16. The Master said, Men of old had three failings, which have, perhaps, died out to-day. Ambitious men of old were not nice; now they are unprincipled. Stern men of old were hard; now they are quarrelsome. Ignorant men of old were straight; now they are false. That is all.

17. The Master said, Smooth words and fawning looks are seldom found with love.

18. The Master said, I hate the ousting of scarlet by purple. I hate the strains of Cheng, confounders of sweet music. I hate a sharp tongue, the ruin of kingdom and home.

19. The Master said, I wish no word were spoken!

Tzu-kung said, Sir, if ye said no word, what could your little children write?

The Master said, What are the words of Heaven? The four seasons pass, the hundred things bear life. What are the words of Heaven?

20. Ju Pei wished to see Confucius. Confucius pleaded sickness; but, as the messenger left his door, he took a lute and sang, so the messenger should hear.

21. Tsai Wo[166] asked about mourning for three years. He thought that one was enough.

If for three years gentlemen forsake courtesy, courtesy must suffer. If for three years they forsake music, music must decay. The old grain passes, the new grain sprouts, the round of woods for the fire-drill is ended in one year.

The Master said, Feeding on rice, clad in brocade, couldst thou be at rest?

---

[164] His son
[165] The first two books of *The Book of Poetry*
[166] A disciple

I could, he answered.

Then do what gives thee rest. But a gentleman, when he is mourning, has no taste for sweets and no ear for music; he cannot rest in his home. So he gives these up. Now, they give thee rest; then keep them.

After Tsai Wo had gone, the Master said, Yü's[167] want of love! At the age of three a child first leaves the arms of his father and mother, and mourning lasts for three years everywhere below heaven. But did Yü have for three years the love of his father and mother?

22. The Master said, It is hard indeed when a man eats his fill all day, and has nothing to task the mind! Could he not play at chequers? Even that were better.

23. Tzu-lu said, Do gentlemen honour daring?

They put right higher, said the Master. With daring and no sense of right gentlemen turn rebels and small men turn robbers.

24. Tzu-kung said, Do gentlemen hate too?

They do, said the Master. They hate the sounding of evil deeds; they hate men of low estate that slander those over them; they hate daring without courtesy; they hate men that are stout and fearless, but blind.

And Tz'u,[168] he said, dost thou hate too?

I hate those that take spying for wisdom, who take want of manners for courage, and take tale-telling for honesty.

25. The Master said, Only maids and serving-lads are hard to train. If we draw near to them, they get unruly; if we hold them off, they grow spiteful.

26. The Master said, When a man of forty is hated, he will be so to the end.

---

[167] Tsai Wo
[168] Tzu-kung

Chapter XVIII

1. The lord of Wei[169] left, the lord of Chi[170] was made a slave, Pi-kan[171] spake out, and died.

    Confucius said, Three of the Yin had love.

2. Whilst Liu-hsia Hui[172] was Chief Knight[173] he was dismissed thrice.

    Men said. Is it not yet time to leave. Sir?

    He answered, If I serve men the straight way, where can I go without being dismissed thrice? If I am to serve men the crooked way, why should I leave the land of my father and mother?

3. Speaking of how to treat Confucius, Ching, Duke of Ch'i, said, I cannot treat him as I do the Chi. I put him between Chi and Meng.

    I am old, he said; I cannot use him.

    Confucius left.

4. The men of Ch'i[174] sent a gift of music girls. Chi Huan accepted them, and for three days no court was held.

    Confucius left.

5. Chieh-yü, the mad-head of Ch'u, as he passed Confucius, sang,

---

[169] Kinsmen of the tyrant Chou Hsin, who brought the house of Yin to an end
[170] Kinsmen of the tyrant Chou Hsin, who brought the house of Yin to an end
[171] Kinsmen of the tyrant Chou Hsin, who brought the house of Yin to an end
[172] See note to Book XV, § 13
[173] Or Criminal Judge
[174] To Lu, 497 b.c. The turning-point in Confucius's career. He left office and his native land, and wandered abroad for twelve long years

Phoenix, bright phoenix,Thy glory is ended!Think of to-morrow;The past can't be mended.Up and away!The Court is todayWith danger attended.

Confucius alighted, for he wished to speak with him: but he hurried away, and he could not speak with him.

6. Ch'ang-chü and Chieh-ni were working in the fields. As Confucius passed them, he sent Tzu-lu to ask for the ford.

Ch'ang-chü said, Who is that holding the reins?

He is K'ung Ch'iu, said Tzu-lu.

Is he K'ung Ch'iu of Lu?

Yes, said Tzu-lu.

He knows the ford, said Ch'ang-chü.

Tzu-lu asked Chieh-ni.

Who are ye, Sir? he answered.

I am Chung Yu.

The disciple of K'ung Ch'iu of Lu?

Yes, he answered.

All below heaven is seething and boiling, said Chieh-ni, who can change it? How much better would it be to follow a knight that flees the world than to follow a knight that flees persons!

And he went on hoeing without stop.

Tzu-lu went and told the Master, whose face fell.

Can I herd with birds and beasts? he said. Whom but these men can I take as fellows? And if the Way were kept by all below heaven, I should not need to change them.

7. Tzu-lu, who was following behind, met an old man carrying a basket on his staff.

Tzu-lu asked him, Have ye seen the Master, Sir?

The old man answered, Thy four limbs are idle, thou canst not sort the five seeds: who is thy Master?

And he planted his staff, and weeded.

Tzu-lu stood and bowed.

He kept Tzu-lu for the night, killed a fowl, made millet, gave them him to eat, and presented his two sons.

Tzu-lu left the next day, and told the Master.

The Master said, He is in hiding.

He sent Tzu-lu back to see him; but when he arrived he had gone.

Tzu-lu said, Not to take office is not right. If the ties of old and young cannot be thrown off, how can he throw off the liege's duty to his lord? He wishes to keep his life clean, but he is unsettling the bonds between men. To discharge that duty a gentleman takes office, though he knows beforehand that the Way will not be kept.

8. Po-yi, Shu-ch'i, Yü-chung, Yi-yi, Chu-chang, Liu-hsia Hui and Shao-lien were men that hid from the world.

The Master said, Po-yi[175] and Shu-ch'i[176] did not bend the will or shame the body.

We must say that Liu-hsia Hui[177] and Shao-lien bent the will and shamed the body. Their words hit man's duty, their deeds hit our hopes. This we can say and no more.

We may say that Yü-chung and Yi-yi lived hidden, but were free of speech. Their lives were clean, their retreat was well weighed.

But I am unlike all of them: there is nothing I must, or must not, do.

9. Chih, the Great Music-master, went to Ch'i; Kan, the conductor at the second meal, went to Ch'u; Liao, the conductor at the third meal, went to Ts'ai; Chüeh, the conductor at the fourth meal, went to Ch'in. The drum master Fang-shu crossed the River; the tambourine master Wu crossed the Han; Yang the second bandmaster and Hsiang, who played the sounding stones, crossed the sea.

10. The Duke of Chou[178] said to the Duke of Lu,[179] A gentleman does not forsake kinsmen, nor offend his great lieges by not using them. He will not cast off an old friend unless he have big cause; he does not ask everything of anyone.

11. Chou had eight knights: Po-ta and Po-kuo, Chung-tu and Chung-hu, Shu-yeh and Shu-hsia, Chi-sui and Chi-kua.

---

[175] See note to Book V, § 22
[176] See note to Book V, § 22
[177] See note to Book XV, § 13
[178] See note to Book VII, § 5
[179] His son

Book XIX

1. Tzu-chang said, The knight that stakes his life when he sees danger, who in sight of gain thinks of right, and whose thoughts are reverent at worship, and sad when he is in mourning, will do.
2. Tzu-hsia said, Goodness, clutched too narrowly; a belief in the Way which is not honest; can they be said to be, or said not to be?
3. The disciples of Tzu-hsia asked Tzu-chang whom we should choose as our companions.

   Tzu-chang said. What does Tzu-hsia say?

   They answered, Tzu-hsia says, If the men be well for thee, go with them; if they be not well, push them off.

   Tzu-chang said. This is not the same as what I had heard. A gentleman honours worth and bears with the many. He applauds goodness and pities weakness. If I were a man of great worth, what could I not bear with in others? If I am without worth, men will push me off: why should I push other men off?

4. Tzu-hsia said, Though there must be things worth seeing along small ways, a gentleman does not follow them, for fear of being left at last in the mire.
5. Tzu-hsia said, He that each day remembers his failings and each month forgets nothing won may be said to love learning indeed!
6. Tzu-hsia said, By wide learning and singleness of will, by keen questions and home thinking we reach love.
7. Tzu-hsia said, To master the hundred trades, apprentices work in a shop; by learning, a gentleman finds his way.
8. Tzu-hsia said, The small man must always gloss his faults.
9. Tzu-hsia said, A gentleman changes thrice. Looking up to him he seems stern; as we draw near, he warms; but his speech, when we hear it, is sharp.
10. Tzu-hsia said, Until they trust him, a gentleman lays no burdens on his people. If they do not trust him, they will think it cruel. Until they trust

him, he does not chide them. Unless they trust him, it will seem fault-finding.

11. Tzu-hsia said, If we keep within the bounds of honour, we can step to and fro through propriety.

12. Tzu-yu said, The disciples, the little sons of Tzu-hsia, can sprinkle and sweep, attend and answer, come in and go out; but what can come of twigs without roots?

1. When Tzu-hsia heard this, he said, Yen Yu[180] is wrong. If we teach one thing in the way of a gentleman first, shall we tire before reaching the next? Thus plants and trees differ in size. Should the way of a gentleman bewilder him? To learn it, first and last, none but the holy are fit.

13. Tzu-hsia said, A servant of the crown should give his spare strength to learning. With his spare strength a scholar should serve the crown.

14. Tzu-yu said, Mourning should stretch to grief, and stop there.

15. Tzu-yu said, Our friend Chang[181] can do hard things, but love is not yet his.

16. Tseng-tzu said, Chang is so spacious, so lordly, that at his side it is hard to do what love bids.

17. Tseng-tzu said, I have heard the Master say, Man never shows what is in him unless it be in mourning those dear to him.

18. Tseng-tzu said, I have heard the Master say, In all else we may be as good a son as Meng Chuang, but in not changing his father's ministers, or his father's rule, he is hard to match.

19. The Meng[182] made Yang Fu[183] Chief Knight,[184] who spake to Tseng-tzu about it.

2. Tseng-tzu said, Those above have lost their way, the people have long been astray. When thou dost get at the truth, be moved to pity, not puffed with joy.

20. Tzu-kung said, Chou[185] was not so very wicked! Thus a gentleman hates to live in a hollow, down into which runs all that is foul below heaven.

21. Tzu-kung said, A gentleman's faults are like the eating of sun or moon.[186] All men see them, and when he mends all men look up to him.

22. Kung-sun Ch'ao of Wei asked Tzu-kung, From whom did Chung-ni[187] learn?

Tzu-kung said, The Way of Wen and Wu[188] has not fallen into ruin. It lives in men: the big in big men, the small in small men. In none of them

---

[180] Tzu-yu
[181] Tzu-chang
[182] The chief of the Meng clan, powerful in Lu
[183] A disciple of Tseng-tzu
[184] Or criminal judge
[185] The tyrant that ended the Yin dynasty
[186] An eclipse
[187] Confucius

is the Way of Wen and Wu missing. How should the Master not learn it? What need had he for a set teacher?

23. In talk with the great men of the court Shu-sun Wu-shu[189] said, Tzu-kung is worthier than Chung-ni.

Tzu-fu Ching-po told this to Tzu-kung.

Tzu-kung said, This is like the palace wall. My wall reaches to the shoulder: peeping over you see the good home within. The Master's wall is several fathoms high: no one can see the beauty of the Ancestral Temple and the wealth of its hundred officers, unless he gets in by the gate. And if only a few men find the gate, may not my lord have spoken the truth?

24. Shu-sun Wu-shu cried down Chung-ni.

Tzu-kung said, It is labour lost. Chung-ni cannot be cried down. The greatness of other men is a hummock, over which we can still leap. Chung-ni is the sun or moon, which no one can overleap. Though the man were willing to kill himself, how could he hurt the sun or moon? That he does not know his own measure would only be seen the better!

25. Ch'en Tzu-ch'in[190] said to Tzu-kung, Ye humble yourself, Sir. In what is Chung-ni your better?

Tzu-kung said, By one word a gentleman shows wisdom, by one word want of wisdom. Words must not be lightly spoken. No one can come up to the Master, as heaven is not to be climbed by steps. If the Master had power in a kingdom, or a clan, the saying would come true, 'What he sets up stands; he shows the way and men go it, he brings peace and they come, he stirs them and they are at one. Honoured in life, he is mourned when dead!' Who can come up to him?

[188] See Introduction
[189] Head of the Meng clan
[190] A disciple of Tzu-kung

Book XX[191]

1. Yao said, Hail to thee, Shun! The count that Heaven is telling falls on thee. Keep true hold of the centre. If there be stress or want within the four seas, the gift of Heaven will pass for ever.

   Shun laid the same commands on Yü.

   T'ang said, I, Thy little child Li, dare to offer this black steer, and dare to proclaim before Thee, Almighty Lord, that I dare not forgive sin, nor keep down Thy ministers. Search them, O Lord, in Thine heart. If Our life be sinful, visit it not upon the ten thousand homesteads. If the ten thousand homesteads sin, the sin is on Our head.

   Chou bestowed great gifts, and good men grew rich.

   'Loving hearts are better than near kinsmen. All the people blame no one but me.'[192]

   He saw to weights and measures, revised the laws, and brought back broken officers. Order reigned everywhere. He revived ruined kingdoms and restored fiefs that had fallen in. All hearts below heaven turned to him. The people's food, burials and worship weighed most with him. His bounty gained the many, his truth won the people's trust, his earnestness brought success, his justice made men glad.

2. Tzu-chang asked Confucius, How should men be governed?

---

[191] This chapter shows the principles on which China was governed in old times. Yao and Shun were the legendary founders of the Chinese Empire, Yü, T'ang, and Chou were the first emperors of the houses of Hsia, Shang and Chou, which had ruled China up till the time of Confucius

[192] Said by King Wu (Chou). The people blamed him for not dethroning at once the tyrant Chou Hsin

The Master said, To govern men we must honour five fair things and spurn four evil things.

Tzu-chang said, What are the five fair things?

The Master said, A gentleman is kind, but not wasteful; he burdens, but he does not embitter; he is covetous, but not greedy; high-minded, but not proud; stern, but not fierce.

Tzu-chang said, What is meant by kindness without waste?

The Master said, To further what furthers the people, is not that kindness without waste? If burdens be sorted to strength, who will grumble? To covet love and get love, is that greed? Few or many, small or great, all is one to a gentleman: he dares not slight any man. Is not this to be high-minded, but not proud? A gentleman straightens his robe and cap, and settles his look. He is severe, and men look up to him with awe. Is not this to be stern, but not fierce?

Tzu-chang said, What are the four evil things?

The Master said, To leave untaught and then kill is cruelty; not to give warning and to expect things to be done is tyranny; to give careless orders and be strict when the day comes is robbery; to be stingy in rewarding men is littleness.

3. The Master said, He that does not know the Bidding cannot be a gentleman. Not to know good form is to have no foothold. Not to know words is to know nothing of men.